ERNAUX

La Place *and* La Honte

Alison S. Fell

Lecturer in French Studies
Lancaster University

London
Grant & Cutler Ltd 2006

ISBN-10: 07293 0449 3
ISBN-13: 978 07293 0449 8

Depósito legal: V. 3.358 - 2006

Printed in Spain by
Artes Gráficas Soler, S.L., Valencia
for
GRANT & CUTLER LTD
55–57 GREAT MARLBOROUGH STREET, LONDON W1F 7AY

I would like to thank the following for their help and advice: Paul Cooke, Roger Little and Edward Welch.

Contents

Prefatory Note	9
Introduction	11
Genre	21
Education and class	38
Language and style	55
Family secrets	70
Bibliography	82

Prefatory Note

The editions of *La Place* and *La Honte* I have used are the Gallimard 'Collection Folio' paperbacks, nos.1722 and 3154. These volumes figure as nos. 4 and 11 in the Select Bibliography, and are referred to throughout the text according to the style (*4*, p.20). References to other works by Ernaux are also to the Folio editions.

1. Introduction

The publication of Annie Ernaux's *La Place* (1983) marked a turning point for its author. While Ernaux's earlier autobiographical novels, *Les Armoires vides* (1974), *Ce qu'ils disent ou rien* (1977) and *La Femme gelée* (1981), had enjoyed modest sales figures, *La Place* became a best seller. Furthermore, commercial success was matched by critical acclaim. *La Place* was awarded the prestigious Prix Renaudot in 1984 and the majority of reviews were enthusiastic. To date, it has sold approximately half a million copies and has been published in sixteen languages. *La Honte* (1997), the other text I shall focus on in this study, has also sold well (over 100,000 copies), although, for reasons I shall explore further, its critical reception has been more mixed. Ernaux is now a relatively well-known literary figure in France, and is frequently interviewed on television and radio. However, in terms of academic engagement with her texts, her work has received more attention in the UK and in North America than in France. Ernaux's direct and apparently straightforward narrative style, her deliberate blurring of literary genres and foregrounding of issues of gender, class and sexuality have meant that her texts do not always sit easily amongst other writers of twentieth and twenty-first century French literature, particularly those considered canonical. But, as I shall argue in this guide, it is precisely the way in which her works challenge preconceived notions of what makes a text 'literary' that constitutes one of the most interesting facets of her writing.

The narrative material and thematic concerns of *La Place* and *La Honte* are immediately familiar to seasoned readers of Ernaux's corpus. In fact, the three autobiographical novels with which she began her literary career contain in condensed form all the principal themes of her work. Denise Lesur and Anne, the adolescent female narrators of *Les Armoires vides* and *Ce qu'ils disent ou rien*, vent their frustration at the limitations constituted by the class and gender norms that have curtailed their sexual and intellectual freedom and have alienated them from their families. The young women are left disillusioned but defiant; their dense, unbroken narratives, written in a direct and informal style, embody a demand to be heard in a society in which linguistic as well as economic differences reflect the prevailing power structures. Similarly, the anonymous first-person narrator of *La Femme gelée* reviews her migration to a higher social class by means of her educational success and marriage in terms of a series of disappointments and disillusionments. As is the case for all of Ernaux's narrators, her experience of social mobility does not lead uncomplicatedly to freedom, intellectual fulfilment, gender equality or personal contentment. Rather, she comes to resent the economic and cultural trappings of privilege that have cut her adrift from her social origins, and have left her feeling psychologically and intellectually 'frozen', as the work's title suggests. The subject matter of these early autobiographical novels is revisited throughout the majority of Ernaux's subsequent publications, the genre of which, as I shall demonstrate in the following chapter, falls somewhere in between biography, autobiography and social history. From *La Place* onwards, Ernaux's writing evolved into what Michael Sheringham terms 'a fusion of autobiography and biography rooted partly in sociological or ethnographic enquiry'. Sheringham notes, further, that in the 1990s Ernaux turned in works such as *'Je ne suis pas sortie de ma nuit'* (1997) and *Journal du dehors* (1993) 'to another form of autobiographical writing, affiliated to the diary' (*56*, p.13). Yet while the forms of her texts have continued to evolve, the themes have remained constant. Ernaux has accordingly been described as an 'écrivain du ressassement', in that her texts revolve around a limited number of key issues which are explored through the recounting and analysis of similar autobiographical narrative material. Such issues include: the difficulties involved in class migration; the process of 'embourgeoisement' through education; language; sexuality and the body; family relationships; the interplay between individuals and society; memory and loss; and writing and identity. Many of Ernaux's works focus more specifically on subjects that have rarely figured, and have even been considered taboo, in literary texts, such as working-class culture, female sexuality, abortion, the effects of Alzheimer's disease, domestic violence and, more recently, breast cancer. The literary treatment of these hitherto outlawed subjects has scandalised some readers, but has frequently struck a chord with others, who find themselves empathising or identifying with Ernaux's narrators. In the following chapters, I will explore key thematic and stylistic elements of *La Place* and *La Honte* in an attempt, on the one hand, to account for their enduring appeal for readers, and, on the other, to consider some of the contradictions and ambiguities of Ernaux's literary project.

The themes I have identified surface, to differing degrees, in *La Place* and *La Honte*. *La Place* begins and ends with accounts of the death of Ernaux's father, which is chronicled in a flat and factual tone: 'Mon père est mort deux mois après [les épreuves pratiques du CAPES], jour pour jour. Il avait soixante-sept ans et tenait avec ma mère un café-alimentation dans un quartier tranquille non loin de la gare, à Y... (Seine-Maritime)' (*4*, p.13). One would expect, perhaps, an account of a parent's death to produce a narrative conveying an intensely private experience of grief and loss. *La Place*, however, considers the author's relationship with her father not primarily in terms of a daughter's bereavement, but in relation to the collective experience of class migration and social exclusion. After an opening section recounting the circumstances of her father's death and funeral, the narrative consists largely of evocations of his past life, and of quasi-sociological examinations of the dominant socio-cultural and political discourses that were circulating in the lower-middle-class milieu in which he lived. Beginning with his family history, the narrator traces the different stages of her father's life: his curtailed education, work as a farm labourer, national service, factory job, marriage, and purchase of a moderately successful small grocery business. We learn too of the evolving nature of the father-daughter relationship. As the daughter succeeds in her studies, she moves into a different social sphere and in consequence her relationship with her father comes under increasing strain: 'J'émigre doucement vers le monde petit-bourgeois [...]. L'univers pour moi s'est retourné' (*4*, p.79). Finally, they become almost like strangers, unable to communicate. Interspersed in the text are also several self-reflexive passages of metanarrative (that is, passages which are separated from and comment upon the main narrative of the father's life) in which Ernaux's narrator raises important questions relating to the methodology and motivations of her writing. It becomes clear that one of her motives for writing is to assuage her guilt for having rejected her father and all he stood for; a desire to understand why they had become estranged. The narrator claims success in having rediscovered her past, and in having revalorised her parents' lives and culture: 'J'ai fini de mettre au jour l'héritage que j'ai dû déposer au seuil du monde bourgeois et cultivé quand j'y suis entrée' (*4*, p.111). The text ends, however, on a more ambiguous note, evoking the daily drudgery of one of the narrator's former students working in a supermarket checkout, a scene to which I will return in the following chapters.

La Honte mirrors the circular structure of *La Place*, in that it begins and ends with the description and analysis of events in the narrator's life that took place in the summer of 1952. Its opening line shockingly recounts an incident which appears initially, like the description of the father's death in *La Place*, to belong to the domain of personal and emotionally intense experience: 'Mon père a voulu tuer ma mère un dimanche de juin, au début de l'après-midi' (*11*, p.13). Again, however, the apparently private experience is universalised, as the father's act of violence and the daughter's subsequent shame are related to wider issues of social class, Catholicism, education and sexuality. As in *La Place*, the narrator returns to her childhood in an attempt to understand the repercussions of her family's socio-economic situation on her later life. In her attempts to rediscover the contours of her family life in 1952, Ernaux's narrator begins by considering photographs that were taken that year, as well as other surviving 'traces matérielles' — postcards of Queen Elizabeth II and Limoges cathedral, a collection of postcards from Lourdes, a red leather sewing kit, some sheet music, and a vesperal (*11*, pp.27–30). She also looks at newspapers from the same year, although she finds little to enlighten her there. Finally, she turns to her own inner 'archive'. She first defines the geographical limits of her twelve-year-old world, the 'topographie d'Y. en 52' (*11*, p.46), before moving on to outline the unspoken codes and rules which regulated the milieu in which her family lived. She also focuses on the forms of language she had at her disposal at the age of twelve, which had a direct effect on the extent to which she was able to express herself. In the next section, the narrator explores the other important structuring element of her young life, her Catholic school, and describes the religious doctrine and social norms that underpinned her education and interaction with her teachers and peers. She concludes that at school individuals were classified according to various religious, social and intellectual criteria, and that in accordance with such classifications her family was found wanting, particularly after she has witnessed her father's act of violence: 'Nous avons cessé d'appartenir à la catégorie des gens corrects' (*11*, p.115). In the final sections of the text, she evokes painful memories of feelings of humiliation when her parents fail to measure up to the expectations inculcated in her by her school. To some extent, she discovers that the scene of her father's rage is not in itself responsible for her lifelong feelings of shame, but had become a kind of cipher for a sense of unworthiness with which she was permanently imbued as a result of her class identity: 'Tout de notre existence est devenu signe de honte' (*11*, p.139).

In many ways, *La Place* and *La Honte* resemble each other. The narrator of *La Honte* wishes to unveil unacknowledged truths or unspoken secrets about her past and her relationship with her father, just as in *La Place* she wishes to confess her daughterly guilt in her acquiescence as an adult with bourgeois discourses that dismissed her father's values and habits. In both texts, evocations of Ernaux's childhood and sociological analyses of historical data are interspersed with sections of metanarrative in which the text's narrator asks searching questions relating to the driving forces and techniques of her literary project. Yet the father-daughter relationship represented in *La Honte* certainly appears, at least at first, to contradict the picture of a gentle and self-effacing father that appears in her earlier work. The text's opening sentence has particular impact for readers familiar with *La Place*, and would appear to undermine the 'truth value' of the judgements and conclusions it contains. It becomes clear, however, as the narrative of *La Honte* develops, that the apparent disparity between the fathers depicted in the two works is not as radical as it may initially appear to be. In both texts, the private relations between father and daughter are revealed to be largely dependent on a broader system of hierarchisation in which one socio-economic group is oppressed by another, dominant group. The father and narrating daughter who appear in Ernaux's 1997 publication do not, therefore, efface their previous incarnations in *La Place*. Rather, they exist in tandem, each adding further layers of meaning to the other. For this reason, in the chapters that follow I tend to treat the texts together, rather than separately, only evoking differences between them where they are directly relevant to my discussion.

La Honte is thus a continuation of the quest begun by the narrator in *La Place*, and the existence of the two texts has important ramifications for an account of the methodology and goals of Ernaux's writing. Her œuvre as a whole can be divided into a number of pairings (*Les Armoires vides/L'Evénement* (2000)*; La Place/La Honte; Une femme* (1988)*/'Je ne suis pas sortie de ma nuit'* (1997); *Passion simple* (1991)*/Se perdre* (2002)) in which the more recent of the two texts offers a re-working, a re-assessment or a previously unpublished account of the particular past experience inscribed in the earlier work. Ernaux has been attacked, particularly in the last ten years, for her tendency to salvage and re-render pre-existing narrative material in her developing autobiographical project. Although the reception of *La Place* and *Une femme* was predominantly positive, reviews of her later publications were more mixed, with many critics expressing a sense of exasperation with her obdurate focus on similar issues in multiple texts, and her increasingly intimate revelations about her past familial and sexual relationships. *La Honte* and *'Je ne suis pas sortie de ma nuit'*, which were published simultaneously and were thus frequently reviewed together, certainly received a less hostile response than one of Ernaux's most controversial publications, *Passion simple* (1991), but nonetheless fifty per cent of the reviews that appeared in the French literary press were negative or mixed. As Lyn Thomas notes, typical criticisms concerned Ernaux's 'obsessive' revisiting of the past, her 'narcissism' and her 'impudeur' (*58*, p.150). Ernaux's continual evocation of the everyday realities — however mundane, however unpleasant — of family and sexual relationships in direct, unadorned prose, has led to accusations that her works are unworthy of the status of literature. Thomas argues that a desire to undermine Ernaux's literary status underpins many of the mixed and negative reviews published in the French press. More specifically, she discusses the tendency of Ernaux's reviewers to compare her with Flaubert's most famous fictional creation, Emma Bovary (a comparison that plays on the fact that both writers set their narratives in the Normandy town of Yvetot). This is discernible in the titles of a number of reviews, such as 'Un gros chagrin. Ou comment dans *Passion simple* Annie Ernaux se prend pour la petite nièce de Madame Bovary' and 'Annie Ernaux: Le bovaryisme est un humanisme'. The latter, a review of *La Honte*, includes the remark 'Madame Bovary, c'est un peu elle' (quoted in *58*, p.155) which makes explicit reference to Flaubert's famous comment that 'Madame Bovary, c'est moi'. While on one level the comparisons of Ernaux's style with that of fellow Norman Flaubert is evidently flattering, given that the latter has one of the safest seats in the French literary hall of fame, Thomas concludes that the insistence on the Ernaux-Bovary association (rather than on a Ernaux-Flaubert connection) also exposes 'the difficulty in French culture of seeing women as writing subjects, rather than objects of the male gaze or textual mastery' (*58*, p.155). Making no distinction between Ernaux-the-writer and Ernaux's first-person narrators, such critics frequently dismiss Ernaux, like Emma Bovary, as a woman whose defective vision of the world leads her to offer a narcissistic, over-sexualised perspective that lacks insight or self-awareness. While it is true that Ernaux's style has become increasingly confessional, her narratives also trace some of the consequences of seeing the world through a flawed ideological lens, and her narrators can rarely be accused of a Bovary-like refusal to reflect on their situation. Comparing Ernaux to Flaubert's literary character, then, is less an illumination of her texts than a means of focusing on her personality rather than on her works, and thus diminishing her literary significance.

Reviews in British and North American journals and newspapers, although by and large less critical, also bear witness to a certain degree of frustration with the increasingly intimate revelations in some of Ernaux's texts and her constant revisiting of the same narrative material. Siobhan McIlvanney's more favourable appraisal of Ernaux's 1997 texts, for example, ends with the 'readerly hope' that Ernaux will 'venture into fresh literary territory' (quoted in *38*, p.61). While it is perhaps not surprising that some readers have found Ernaux's generic ambiguity and direct narrative style alienating, and her tendency to produce texts that constantly return to the same key periods in the narrator's life vexing, it is clear that the existence of dual versions of events, individuals and relationships in Ernaux's corpus is not due simply to writerly vanity or to a drought of fresh ideas or subjects. Rather, they have a specific function in her continuing quest for 'truth' in her literary output. Several recent critical analyses of Ernaux's œuvre argue that her writings implicitly reject the notion that the complexities of identity and interpersonal relationships can be rendered within the limits of a single written text. Fabrice Thumerel notes, for instance, that '[Ernaux] ne croit pas en une possible analyse d'un moi stable dans un récit cohérent' (*59*, p.21). Ernaux's narrator confirms this analysis in the opening pages of *'Je ne suis pas sortie de ma nuit'*, stating that: 'Je crois maintenant que l'unicité, la cohérence auxquelles aboutit une œuvre — quelle que soit par ailleurs la volonté de prendre en compte les données les plus contradictoires — doivent être mis en danger toutes les fois que c'est possible' (*10*, p.13). The two published accounts of the father-daughter relationship in Ernaux's corpus succeed in challenging the 'coherence' and 'unity' potentially supplied by *La Place*, and create together a more subtle and ambiguous picture not only of the individuals concerned and of the class structures that made up their world, but equally of the author's motivations in writing about them. Reading *La Honte*, in other words, leads us necessarily to re-consider and re-assess certain aspects of *La Place*, and the same is true in reverse. Siobhan McIlvanney agrees in her study of Ernaux's writings that: 'While *La Honte* can be viewed as a return to origins in its re-presentation of the constituents of social class in the narrator's childhood and of the shame associated with her working-class upbringing, its content does not simply duplicate the subject matter of existent texts but leads to a reappraisal of it' (*45*, p.154). In an interview discussing *La Honte*, Ernaux suggests that she needs in her writing to '(re)prendre un thème, une période, déjà présents dans mes textes et de les soumettre à une autre approche, constamment. Comme si la "vérité" ne pouvait être obtenue que dans ces mouvements "tournants"' (*26*, p.147). If, then, some kind of 'truth' or authenticity about power structures in French society, about her past, her family relationships and her own identity is a constant goal in Ernaux's writing, it is equally acknowledged as one attainable only through constantly shifting perspectives, through deliberately overturning traditional methods of autobiographical enquiry, and through mercilessly questioning the writer's own potential blind-spots.

Ernaux is keen to emphasise in *La Honte* that she is only ever able to discover a partial truth about the identity of her childhood self: 'La femme que je suis en 95 est incapable de se replacer dans la fille de 52 qui ne connaissait que sa petite ville, sa famille et son école privée, n'avait à sa disposition qu'un lexique réduit' (*11*, p.39). If the process of writing offers Ernaux a perspective on her past that allows her to locate the source of her 'shame' in 1950s socio-cultural discourses, such a perspective is not represented as one that has any more claims to the 'truth' of the self than any other narrative perspective. The revelations about her childhood self and her relationship with her father she makes via her journey into her past in *La Honte* serve to pluralise her representations of self and other. In her writing, Ernaux does not view identity as a given, as an essence to be unveiled, but as a process. This is why she produces multiple versions of her past, and refuses to limit herself to an established literary genre. In the following chapters I will concentrate in more depth on the various ways in which Ernaux carries out her quest to discover truths about her past, beginning with a consideration of the evolving genre of her work.

2. Genre

La Place constitutes a turning point for Ernaux not just because it sold well, but also because it was the first work to be written in her distinctive unadorned style and to straddle a number of different fictional and non-fictional genres. The line between fiction and autobiography had become increasingly blurred with the publication of each of the early autobiographical novels, signalled by the greater degree of anonymity of their narrators. But with *La Place*, Ernaux abandoned the novel form altogether. She turned instead to a hybrid form that combines elements of autobiographical enquiry with techniques of non-fictional genres such as sociology, ethnography and social history. Accordingly, Ernaux situates her writing published since *La Place* 'à la jointure du familial et du social, du mythe et de l'histoire' (*6*, p.23) or as 'quelque chose entre la littérature, la sociologie et l'histoire' (*6*, p.106). The hybrid form of her texts has compelled critics to coin new terms in an attempt to find an appropriate generic label for them, such as 'ethno-autobiography', 'autosocioanalysis' (*35*, p.101) and 'autosocio-biographie' (*59*, p.21). Her work collapses traditional distinctions between autobiography and biography, and between recounting remembered individual experiences and writing collective history. Ernaux's blurring of genre boundaries in this way is a conscious literary strategy on her part. In an interview given in 1992, for example, she comments: 'j'ai ce désir, je crois, de transgresser les formes établies. Quand je cherche à dire quelque chose de vraiment très fort, il faut que la forme éclate aussi d'une certaine manière; on ne peut pas faire autrement' (quoted in *45*, p.4). For Ernaux, the form and content of her literary texts are inescapably interconnected. Just as the form of *La Place* and *La Honte* spans the literary and non-literary, so the subjects of her texts are represented via narrative perspectives that shift between personal, emotional response and dispassionate, objective analysis. Ernaux's refusal to be 'enfermée dans un genre' (*23*, p.148) stems from a desire to position her writing at the intersection between 'public' and 'private' modes of discourse — a desire which is at the heart of her literary project. In this chapter I will explore the hybrid form of *La Place* and *La Honte* in more detail. I shall discuss, first, those genre boundaries that are crossed by the texts. This will lead to a consideration of the implications of the texts' form for Ernaux's aims as a writer. Finally, I shall illustrate my discussion of the significance of Ernaux's formal innovations with an examination of her descriptions of various photographs. The commentaries on family photographs offered by Ernaux's narrators in *La Place* and *La Honte* neatly demonstrate how her blurring of genres allows her to bring together different and alternating perspectives on a past reality in a way not possible within the bounds of many traditional literary forms.

In a section of metanarrative in the opening pages of *La Place*, Ernaux's narrator describes her disillusionment with the novel form in her initial attempts to write about her relationship with her father after his death: 'Par la suite, j'ai commencé un roman dont il était le personnage principal. Sensation de dégoût au milieu du récit. Depuis peu, je sais que le roman est impossible' (*4*, pp.23–24). She began, as she confirms in another essay, to see the novel as 'une sorte de tricherie' (*17*, p.221). The reason Ernaux rejects any fictionalisation of her father's identity relates to her ambivalent relationship to what she considers to be the middle-class world of literature. For Ernaux, the novel is essentially a bourgeois genre. This is problematic for a narrative focusing on her father's life for two reasons. Firstly, she argues that novelistic discourse was alien to her father who, despite his economic ascension to the lower middle classes was still, at least to some extent, a product of his working-class roots. We are told in *La Place* for example that he only understood the French word 'culture' as an agricultural term: 'Il a toujours appelé [la culture] le travail de la terre, l'autre sens de culture, le spirituel, lui était inutile' (*4*, p.34). The term's other meaning, related to the domain of 'le spirituel', was inextricably linked to the bourgeois trappings of 'high' culture — novels, poetry, philosophy and so on — and belonged to an elevated realm that was remote from her father's experiences and consciousness. Secondly, Ernaux finds the content of the novel as 'impossible' as its form. She considers the novel inappropriate as a vehicle with which to write about her past because, she argues, the novel has often been the source of *mis*representations of the lower classes. It is for this reason that Ernaux does not wish to align herself with other celebrated twentieth-century French novelists such as Marcel Proust and François Mauriac. Their depictions of working-class life at the beginning of the twentieth century do not correspond to what she knows of her father's childhood (*4*, p.29). Rather, Proust's delight in the dialectical French spoken by Françoise, the maid of his novel's narrator, betrays the novelist's unthinking acceptance of upper middle-class norms and values: 'Proust relevait avec ravissement les incorrections et les mots anciens de Françoise. Seule l'esthétique lui importe parce que Françoise est sa bonne et non sa mère' (*4*, p.62). For Ernaux, the novel form is incapable of representing the truth of her past or of her parents' lives. Its adoption, rather, would risk reducing her father's identity, and their relationship, to a series of bourgeois literary clichés. Ernaux's abandonment of the novel is thus intimately related to a central preoccupation of her work — the devaluing or exclusion of the lower classes by the hegemonic cultural values of the ruling classes.

If its bourgeois associations lead Ernaux definitively to reject the novel, it is equally difficult to place her texts confidently under the heading of any other genre. This is true, for example, of the genre of autobiography, which seems on the face of it to be a more likely possibility. On one level, Ernaux's narratives are certainly autobiographical. Her life provides the essential narrative raw material from which she constructs her texts. Moreover, the narrating 'I' can be largely identified as the textual avatar or 'double' of the author. As Ernaux confirmed in a recent interview, the 'je' who narrates her autobiographical *récits* can be described as a '"je" complètement assumé, le "je" de la narratrice qui renvoie à Annie Ernaux, écrit sur la couverture' (*26*, p.145). Ernaux's autobiographical narrators, then, conform to Philippe Lejeune's hypothesis of the 'pacte autobiographique' that is established in autobiographies between author-narrator and reader. There are, however, many elements of *La Place* and *La Honte* that do not resemble 'true' autobiography as defined by Lejeune. Ernaux's textual reconstructions of her past do not, for instance, correspond to his well-known definition of autobiography as a 'récit rétrospectif en prose qu'une personne réelle fait de sa propre existence, lorsqu'elle met l'accent sur sa vie individuelle, en particulier sur l'histoire de sa personnalité'[1] since, as Marie-France Savéan points out, 'le personnage principal d[u] récit n'est pas l'auteur-narrateur et […] il ne s'agit pas de l'histoire d'une personnalité' (55, p.20). Rather, Ernaux's texts have a dual focus. In *La Place* and *La Honte* her autobiographical enquiry concentrates as much on her parents' lives as it does on her own. This ambiguity is further heightened by the works' titles. Does 'la place' refer to the uncomfortable social position of the father who has left behind a rural background to become a 'petit commerçant', or to that of the daughter who has similarly migrated, this time to the bourgeoisie? Is 'la honte' the father's shame in relation to his perceived social inferiority, or the daughter's shame at his act of violence? The open-ended nature of the titles' significations is by no means accidental. It is not simply a question of choosing between the labels 'biography' or 'auto-biography' in relation to Ernaux's works. Indeed, the former is no more satisfactory than the latter, as for Ernaux the position of biographer is as problematic as that of novelist. Writing a biography, particularly of a person known as intimately as a parent, can tend towards hagiography or, at the opposite extreme, denunciation. In her writing, Ernaux does not wish either to sentimentalise or condemn her parents' existence, but is attempting, like a detective, to seek out a truth (and not *the* truth) about their lives and, concomitantly, to discover new insights into her own identity.

By intermingling elements of biography and autobiography, *La Place* and *La Honte* point to a core belief frequently expressed in

---

[1] Philippe Lejeune, *Le Pacte autobiographique* (Paris: Seuil, 1975), p.14.

Ernaux's writing. Unlike many traditional autobiographers, Ernaux argues that truth about the self is not to be discovered via the charting of an inward and solo journey of discovery. Authenticity in Ernaux's inscriptions of selfhood is, rather, shown to be attainable only by situating the self in relation to the others that impinge on an individual's existence. That this is the case is emphasised in *Journal du dehors*, a collection of diary entries detailing her everyday encounters and experiences in an anonymous suburb of Paris. Ernaux, as narrating 'I', writes:

> Je suis sûre maintenant qu'on se découvre soi-même davantage en se projetant dans le monde extérieur que dans l'introspection du journal intime — lequel, né il y a deux siècles, n'est pas forcément éternel. Ce sont les autres, anonymes côtoyés dans le métro, les salles d'attente, qui, par l'intérêt, la colère ou la honte dont ils nous traversent, réveillent notre mémoire et nous révèlent à nous-mêmes. (*8*, p.10)

Ernaux points here to the significance of the epigraph to *Journal du dehors*, taken from Jean-Jacques Rousseau: 'Notre vrai moi n'est pas tout entier en nous'. Our 'true' self, in other words, is not situated within, at the centre of the mind or soul, and it cannot be straightforwardly reconstituted through the process of writing. Rather, the locus of identity is *dehors*, where self and other, private and public interact. To put it another way, individual subjectivity in Ernaux's work is inescapably intertwined and interspersed with the subjectivities of others. From this perspective, the dividing line traditionally drawn between autobiography and biography is an artificial one, since no individual exists in isolation from others. This leads Lyn Thomas to suggest that a more appropriate term for Ernaux's work is 'auto/biography', which emphasises the 'lack of clear boundaries between biography and autobiography' (*58*, p.30).[2]

---

[2] Lyn Thomas borrows the term 'auto/biography' from Laura Marcus, who adopts it in her study *Auto/biographical Discourses: Theory, Criticism, Practice* (Manchester: Manchester University Press, 1994).

In *La Place* and *La Honte*, there exists simultaneously a first-person autobiographical narrator and a third-person biographical narrated subject, and these are presented as interrelated and interdependent entities.

Although 'auto/biography' may be a more appropriate categorisation of *La Place* and *La Honte* than novel, biography or autobiography, the term plays down the ethnographic thrust of Ernaux's writing. Her understanding of the self as inevitably bound up in the identities of others is not restricted to her family relationships, but refers equally to the wider social relations in which each of us engages on a daily basis. Ernaux's interest in the lives and experiences of her own family is motivated in part by a desire to link such individual experiences with collective social movements and phenomena. In Siobhan McIlvanney's terms, 'Ernaux's auto/ biographical writing repeatedly highlights the representative elements of both her narrators' existence and those with whom they come into contact' (*45*, p.5). The titles of *La Place* and *La Honte*, for instance, not only underline the blurring of the lines between biography and autobiography, but their generic status (signalled by the use of the definite article) also intimates the extent to which she wishes her personal experiences to have a more universal significance. This aspect of Ernaux's work is underscored by the fact that the French 'place' is equivalent to the Greek 'agora' and the Latin 'forum', which designate a public space for the exchange of both goods and ideas. Ernaux's work is thereby set up as a site of engagement with wider public discourses; it is not just the social positioning and shame of a particular father and/or daughter that is at stake, but that of a whole sector of the French population, which the narrator analyses in the guise of a sociologist or ethnographer. Thus, if one takes into account the author's ethnographic intentions, it does not come as a surprise that *La Place* was originally to have been entitled *Eléments pour une ethnologie familiale*.

The narrator of *La Place* outlines her aims and objectives early on in the narrative: 'Je rassemblerai les paroles, les gestes, les goûts de mon père, les faits marquants de sa vie, tous les signes objectifs d'une existence que j'ai aussi partagée' (*4*, p.24). At this point in the text, Ernaux assigns herself the role of a sociologist or semiologist, collating the 'objective signs' of her father's existence, rather than the more traditional one of novelist, memorialist or sentimental biographer. The sociological status of the text is reinforced by the way in which the father's life is used as a means of reconstructing a social history of France from the late nineteenth century until the 1970s. The narrator alludes in the course of her narrative to historical events (such as the two world wars) and socio-economic trends (such as the rise of the *hypermarché* and consequent demise of the small grocery shop) that brought about widespread social change. The changing jobs and locations of three generations of her family are similarly put forward as an illustrative case-study of the way in which France, like other European nations in the nineteenth and twentieth centuries, developed from an agrarian to an urban, industrial economy. Thus, while her grandparents worked on the land or in cottage industries, her father, after beginning his working life as a farm labourer, moved to work in the factory where her mother was also employed, and then after his marriage set up a *café-épicerie* with his wife. His daughter, of course, completed the family's progress from the rural working classes to the urban middle classes by becoming a writer and teacher.

At times, Ernaux adopts a similarly sociological/ethnographic perspective in *La Honte*: 'Naturellement pas de récit, qui produirait une réalité au lieu de la chercher. Ne pas me contenter non plus de lever et transcrire les images du souvenir mais traiter celles-ci comme des documents qui s'éclaireront en les soumettant à des approches différentes. Etre en somme ethnologue de moi-même' (*11*, p.40). This time the subject under scrutiny is not her father but her childhood self. The research into her past self is conducted with methodical determination. She begins by consulting documents of the period (including newspapers, photographs, postcards and song lyrics) before analysing the language of the child she once was in an attempt to 'retrouver les mots avec lesquels je me pensais et pensais le monde autour' (*11*, p.39). Ernaux's quest in *La Place* and *La*

Honte to construct an authentic account of her lower-middle-class roots often appears to lead her to trust objective 'facts' more than subjective memories, which run the risk of over-dependence on emotional response, and encourage a false conception of the self as possessing an unchanging 'core' or 'soul' that survives an ever-evolving socio-economic context intact. To exemplify this, Ernaux contrasts her method of autobiographical enquiry in *La Honte* with Proust's notion of involuntary memory, arguing that whereas Proust's evoked memories convinced him of the 'permanence de la personne', for her 'la mémoire n'apporte aucune preuve de [sa] permanence ou de [son] identité'. For Ernaux, memory tends to confirm not the Proustian 'moi permanent', but the 'fragmentation' and 'historicité' of her individual subjectivity (*11*, p.102).

Ernaux frequently affirms her appropriation of the detached and dispassionate gaze of a social historian or ethnographer in interviews, claiming in 1998, for example: 'je me sers de cette matière autobiographique comme un scientifique ferait d'un objet qu'il étudie et dont il se sert pour aller vers autre chose' (*23*, p.142). However, as I have already implied, we should hesitate before unquestioningly accepting the 'objectivity' of Ernaux's accounts of her past experiences and relationships. Certainly, on one level, the materialist understanding of identity that underpins her work leads her to attempt to distance herself from her narrative subjects, to analyse her parents and herself as social subjects rather than focusing on specific personality traits or the particular dynamics of their relationship. But while Ernaux's narrators foreground a desire for a certain kind of social realism, her texts also make the reader aware of the inevitable failure of the narrator's attempts to write from a position of pure objectivity. In *La Place*, for instance, the paradox inherent in her methodology is explicitly acknowledged:

> En m'efforçant de révéler la trame significative d'une vie dans un ensemble de faits et de choix, j'ai l'impression de perdre au fur et à mesure la figure particulière de mon père. L'épure tend à prendre toute la place, l'idée à courir toute seule. Si au contraire je laisse

> glisser les images du souvenir, je le revois tel qu'il était,
> son rire, sa démarche, il me conduit par la main à la
> foire et les manèges me terrifient, tous les signes d'une
> condition partagée avec d'autres me deviennent indiffé-
> rents. (*4*, p.45)

Here, Ernaux's narrator refers to the existence of an alternative
perspective on her father, one precisely based on subjective memory
and emotional response. This conflict between objective and
subjective points of view in relation to the past is equally important
in *La Honte*, where the personal trauma — 'ce tsunami psychique'
(*61*, p.133) — engendered by her father's act of violence is recorded
along with its connections to broader social realities. However,
rather than omitting the complex nature of her position brought
about by the inevitable oscillation in her narrative representations
between (objective, socio-historic, documentary) 'public' and
(subjective, emotional) 'private' perspectives, Ernaux records it in
both texts as an integral part of the writing process. Her narrators do
not present their narratives as impersonal and factual history
textbooks, but articulate an awareness of the texts as 'un ensemble
de faits et de choix', as an inevitably subjective selection of facts
and memories. This recognition of the complex interaction of
objective and subjective perspectives, of fact and fiction, is
underscored in the penultimate paragraph of *La Honte*:

> Durant les mois où j'ai écrit ce livre, j'étais tout de suite
> alertée par les faits, quels qu'ils soient — sortie d'un
> film, d'un livre, mort d'un artiste, etc. — , dont on
> signalait qu'ils s'étaient passés en 1952. Il me semblait
> qu'ils certifiaient la réalité de cette année lointaine et de
> mon être d'enfant. Dans un livre de Shohei Ooka, *Les
> Feux*, paru au Japon en 1952, je lis: "Tout ceci n'est
> peut-être qu'une illusion mais je ne puis mettre en doute
> ce que j'ai ressenti. Le souvenir aussi est une
> expérience". (*11*, p.141)

The implied admission that her ethnographic research into her past may be, in the end, insufficient is accompanied by a plea for the authenticity of her subjective experience. The inclusion of the quotation thereby inevitably undermines any claims to pure, unadulterated truth implied by the objective, pseudo-scientific persona that she occasionally adopts in her writing, and highlights the importance of emotional response and individual recollection in the quest for truth, however unreliable and open to doubt.

Although, then, Ernaux often draws attention to her texts' focus on the public, representational aspects of her family history, her narrators do not attempt to hide the ways in which her historical/sociological/ethnographical analysis is to some degree an artificial construct. The narrator's role as an objective observer of historical data is always, inevitably, fused with her other roles as woman, daughter and writer of literary texts, and the taking on of different perspectives or 'voices' in this way is, as Ernaux herself confirms, a crucial element of her writing: '[Le] "je": avant tout, c'est une *voix*. [...] La voix peut avoir toutes sortes de tonalités, violente, hurlante, ironique, histrionne, tentatrice (textes érotiques), etc. Elle peut s'imposer, devenir spectacle, ou s'effacer devant les faits qu'elle raconte, jouer sur plusieurs registres ou rester dans la monodie' (*21*, p.30). For Ernaux, writing about her parents' lives inevitably involves problematic and irresolvable interaction between public and private voices, between historical truth, emotional truth and literary representation. It is, in effect, the combination of elements from different genres that allows her to demonstrate the connections that exist between the individual and society, between her father's life and the collective experiences of his generation and class in twentieth-century France.

Finally, I would like to highlight the layering in this way of public and private meanings in Ernaux's work by discussing the several photographs that are described in *La Place* and *La Honte*. On the one hand, references to photographic 'evidence' in Ernaux's texts seek to underline the objectivity and historical authenticity of the author's politically motivated, public narrative perspective. Acting as a kind of investigative social historian, Ernaux's narrator decodes the family photographs, treating them as historical documents which provide the reader with evidence relating to the social condition of the lower classes in twentieth-century France. On the other, the photographs also function as symbolic representations of the individual, private dynamics of her family relationships. It is interesting, for example, that Ernaux chooses not to include copies of the photographs in her published works. It is as if there needs to be something hidden from public consumption, something that can remain private and perhaps inexplicable. This is reminiscent of Roland Barthes's *La Chambre claire* (1980), a text which is at once a theory of photography and a personal act of mourning for his mother.[3] Barthes, like Ernaux, does not consider photographs to be neutral representations of the individuals they feature. Rather, he argues that they are charged with multiple meanings for the viewer to decipher. Barthes distinguishes between what he calls the 'studium' and the 'punctum' of a photograph. The studium is its culturally coded meaning, understandable to all viewers within a particular ideological context as it is part of a collective social symbolism. The punctum, in contrast, is something that 'punctures' or 'pierces' an individual viewer, and lies outside of shareable codes. The punctum, then, cannot be communicated as it is precisely incommunicable, and for this reason Barthes does not include a particular photograph of his mother — the 'Winter Garden photograph' — that he claims contains her 'essence'. Barthes and Ernaux have much in common in their analysis of photographs. Like Barthes, Ernaux is interested in the ideological connotations of images that are falsely assumed to be 'natural' or 'neutral' representations of reality. In an essay written to accompany an album of photographs of twentieth-century French workers, for example, Ernaux describes her reactions to the individuals photographed: 'Des êtres anonymes, vivant dans un temps où je n'existais pas encore, et qui pourtant me bouleversent: je les reconnais. Je veux dire que leurs corps, leurs postures, leurs gestes,

---

[3] Roland Barthes, *La Chambre claire: note sur la photographie* (Paris: Gallimard, 1980).

font partie de mon héritage. [Les photos] renvoie[nt] aux structures économiques de la société' (*18*, pp.44–45). In *La Place* and *La Honte* she likewise offers an analysis of the coded social meanings, or 'studium', of individual photographs. At the same time, she suggests that these are not the only meanings with which photographs are charged. Although it is the ideological connotations of the photographs that are foregrounded by her narrators, it is also possible to interpret a 'private' dimension, a dimension that is underplayed by the text, but is nevertheless present. Yet as Barthes notes, the 'punctum' of a particular image, that is, the emotional impact a photograph has on a particular viewer, is in the final analysis impossible to articulate. To expose family photographs to public view in a published text, especially one that includes a written analysis of them, risks limiting the images to one particular, shareable set of connotations. It is perhaps to avoid reducing her family photographs to the everyday, to the banal, and thus ridding them of their emotional charge, that led Ernaux to decide that they should remain unpublished.

La Place and La Honte contain descriptions of seven photographs, which are described at strategic points throughout the texts. The photographs vary between professional portraits of family members taken on important occasions and snapshots taken on holiday or in the garden of the 'café-épicerie' in which the family lived. They are used, firstly, as a means by which the author is able to sketch out the contours of a lower-middle-class existence. It becomes clear that in the narrator's childhood photographs were formal, awkward and posed affairs, rather than the more 'spontaneous' and smiling family photographs with which her bourgeois readers may be more familiar. In one of the photographs described in *La Place*, for example, her father is typically unsmiling and appears uncomfortable, dressed in his Sunday best: 'Alentour de la cinquantaine, encore la force de l'âge, la tête très droite, l'air soucieux, comme s'il craignait que la photo ne soit ratée, il porte un ensemble, pantalon foncé, veste claire sur une chemise et une cravate. Photo prise un dimanche, en semaine, il était en bleus' (*4*, p.55). In her family's milieu, photographs were taken only infrequently, to celebrate landmarks such as a marriage or christening, or as confirmations of the material success of the photograph's subject: 'On se fait photographier avec ce qu'on est fier de posséder, le commerce, le vélo, plus tard la 4 CV, sur le toit de laquelle il appuie une main, faisant par ce geste remonter exagérément son veston' (*4*, pp.55–56). The use of 'on' in the above quotation emphasises the representative quality of such photographs; the narrator is speaking primarily as a former member of her parents' class. In similar vein, the photograph discovered in the father's wallet of a group of work colleagues is described as a 'photo typique des livres d'histoire pour "illustrer" une grève ou le Front populaire' (*4*, p.22). The father is cast in this example as a representative of a particular social reality (that is, socio-political life in the 1920s and 1930s), rather than as an individual who enjoys an intimate relationship with the viewer.

In *La Honte*, the narrator details the ways in which the studio photograph of her as a twelve-year-old dressed for communion is equally expressive of her time and socio-cultural milieu. It is analysed as an elaborate construct made to connote asexual innocence and religious piety:

> Elle est agenouillée sur un prie-dieu, les coudes sur l'appui rembourré, les mains, larges, avec une bague à l'auriculaire, jointes sous la joue et entourées d'un chapelet qui retombe sur le missel et les gants posés sur le prie-dieu. Caractère flou, informe, de la silhouette dans la robe de mousseline dont la ceinture a été nouée lâche, comme le bonnet. (*11*, p.23)

Following the conventions of traditional portraiture, the kneeling girl is pictured with items of religious symbolism (ring, rosary, prayer book) and her body is camouflaged in a bid to make her portrait conform to a vision of Marian purity. The high quality of the photograph, which is described as a 'photographie d'art', indicates the dominant influence of and continuing respect for the Catholic church in the young girl's community. Likewise, the description of the parents' wedding photograph in *La Place* emphasises not the couple's individuality, but the extent to which they are made to conform to the conventions of the day. They are dressed according to 1930s fashions, and their pose mimes the patriarchal roles of breadwinner and housewife:

> Sur la photo du mariage, on voit les genoux [de la mère]. Elle fixe durement l'objectif sous le voile qui lui enserre le front jusqu'au-dessus des yeux. Elle ressemble à Sarah Bernhardt. Mon père se tient debout à côté d'elle, une petite moustache et "le col à manger de la tarte". Ils ne sourient ni l'un ni l'autre. (*4*, p.37)

In Claire-Lise Tondeur's terms, 'le couple s'est fait faire le document obligatoire qui doit conserver la mémoire de ce jour unique' (*60*, p.79). The description of the wedding photograph, however, hints at more than the rituals undergone by pre-war French lower-middle-class couples. It is the wife rather than the husband whose gaze is hard and determined, which undermines the traditional division of power suggested by their pose. Such an interpretation is further suggested to the reader by the placing of the description of the photograph immediately after a portrait of the narrator's mother as 'une ouvrière vive, répondeuse. Une de ses phrases favorites: "Je vaux bien ces gens-là"' (*4*, p.37). As we read on, it becomes increasingly clear that the relationship between the narrator's parents tends to reverse the traditional roles allotted to husband and wife. In terms of their parental responsibilities, for example, it is the mother who is the vocal, forceful and ambitious disciplinarian, whereas the father fulfils a more nurturing role for his daughter, preparing her meals and picking her up from school. Similar suggestions of the individual dynamics of the family relationships can be found in the descriptions of photographs featuring the narrator and her father. The final photograph described in *La Place* shows the narrator as a sexualised adolescent: 'Sans doute n'ai-je pas encore de notions esthétiques. Je sais toutefois paraître à mon avantage: tournée de trois quarts pour estomper les hanches moulées dans une jupe étroite, faire ressortir la poitrine, une mèche de cheveux balayant le front. Je souris pour me faire l'air doux' (*4*, p.78). The father appears only as a shadow in the background: 'Dans le bas, l'ombre portée du buste de mon père qui a pris la photo' (*4*, p.78). The foregrounding of the daughter in the father-daughter relation here is also evident earlier in the text, when we learn that the group photograph of workers in her father's wallet is inserted behind a newspaper cutting of the narrator's exam results. Both examples symbolise the increasing distance between father and daughter as she proceeds up the educational ladder. Furthermore, the juxtaposition in the text of the final photograph of the body-conscious adolescent with an incident in which the daughter sees her father reading a 'livre obscène' highlights the theme of sexuality in the novel — the secrecy and shame surrounding the body and sexual relations being one of the key areas of conflict in the daughter's growing alienation from her family. The photographs taken in 1952 described in *La Honte* similarly illustrate both the daughter's upward social mobility (she wishes increasingly to resemble 'des gens chics' in contrast to the father's habitual 'air anxieux qu'il a sur toutes les photos': *11*, p.25) and the centrality of issues of sexuality. The two images (the narrator's communion photograph and the photograph taken on holiday with her father in Biarritz) are set up as 'before and after' photographs in relation to the daughter's loss of innocence as a witness to her father's murderous rage and, obliquely, to her burgeoning sexuality that was evidently in conflict with a Catholic interpretation of female behavioural norms. Nancy Miller offers the following analysis of the pairing of images: 'Ernaux reads the two photographs as bookends that hold the closing days of childhood innocence: the one, the good little Catholic girl, the other, the girl who no longer coincides with the child posing in good faith. The second photograph marks the beginning of the time defined by shame, the time after which shame forever becomes her' (*48*, p.41). This shame, as the two photographs chosen for analysis by the narrator demonstrates, is at once social and sexual (I shall return to the interplay between social and sexual shame in Chapter 5). It is significant in this respect that the final paragraph in *La Honte* describes the narrator once again looking at the holiday snapshot taken in 1952. She suggests here that the distance she feels from the girl in the photograph is due not only to the passage of time, but to her subsequent acceptance of the centrality of sexual desire in her conception of self (*11*, p.142). To sum up, in *La Place* and *La Honte* photographs act as 'public' historical sources. They function as material traces of the codes and practices that structured the lives of a particular set of individuals within one echelon of twentieth-century French society. But, more than this, their positioning in the narrative and their description and analysis by the narrator play a significant role in the 'private' narrative of the father-daughter relationship. The father is at once a representative of his time and class, and a key player in his daughter's evolving sense of self. The descriptions of photographs in Ernaux's texts thereby make an important contribution to both the ethnographic-sociological aims of the text, and to the auto/biographical account of the narrator's past life and relationships.

While critics have resorted to neologisms in an attempt to account for the unusual form of *La Place* and *La Honte*, Ernaux is resistant to her works being straightforwardly categorised under a particular heading: 'Je refuse l'appartenance à un genre précis' (*17*, p.221). Her reluctance to allow her texts to be classified within the confines of traditional genre boundaries is closely related to her desire to combine narrative perspectives that are at once personal and impersonal, subjective and objective, to her understanding of the collective roots of individual identity and, equally, to her rejection of bourgeois literary traditions. It is her denunciation of the conventions of various pre-existing literary forms that allows Ernaux to venture into new fields in her work, such as social history, sociology and ethnography, while remaining within the confines of the 'literary'. Traditional forms such as the novel proved inappropriate for the themes she wanted to tackle. In contrast, hybrid forms, as Ernaux notes in an interview, grant her unparalleled and creatively productive freedom: 'Par rapport à la forme du roman de mes débuts, j'ai l'impression d'une immense et, naturellement, terrible liberté. Un horizon s'est dégagé en même temps que je refusais la fiction, toutes les possibilités de forme se sont ouvertes' (*21*, p.21). Like many late twentieth and early twenty-first-century authors, Ernaux rejects the novel, the mainstay of French literary prose since the second quarter of the nineteenth century, in favour of a fusion of different genres, which allows her narrators to speak in multiple voices, the alternation between which corresponds to her desire to offer competing perspectives on the same past narrative event. And it is only by viewing the past through diverse and shifting optics that Ernaux's narrator is able to arrive at the more authentic and satisfying representations of her parents and her past self that she seeks.

3. Education and class

One of the reasons why so many of Ernaux's readers claim to empathise with her narrators in *La Place* and *La Honte* is that they tell the story of a reasonably common experience in post-war France: the difficulties encountered when migrating from one class to another by means of educational achievement. Thierry Poyet notes, for instance, that: 'plusieurs générations jusqu'à une date récente ont connu la généralisation et l'allongement de la scolarisation comme une vraie opportunité de promotion sociale. [...] [*La Place*] devient pour eux un miroir, il dit les vérités de leur vie et traduit en mots tout ce qu'ils n'ont peut-être jamais su exprimer' (*52*, p.47). After the Second World War, the French government enshrined its educational ideals in the 'Préambule' to its 1946 Constitution: 'La nation garantit l'égal accès de l'enfant et de l'adulte à l'instruction, à la formation professionnelle et à la culture.'[4] This was followed in 1947 by the publication of the Langevin-Wallon plan, which again defined the goal of state education as the promotion of the maximum development for the individual child regardless of his or her social origins, and in the 1950s by a number of legal measures designed to facilitate equal access, such as the provision of state bursaries. Ernaux's success in the French higher education system is, like that of other academically gifted children in the 1950s and 1960s, a direct result of these educational policies. In fact, Ernaux's auto/biography can be read as a success story, the tale of a French family's progress over two generations from illiterate grandfather to celebrated writer. However, Ernaux's narrator in *La Place* reveals her academic accomplishments to have been decidedly double-edged in their

---

[4] Quoted in Antoine Prost, *Histoire de l'enseignement en France 1800–1967* (Paris: Presses universitaires de France, 1972), p.95.

effects. As a university graduate, she necessarily enters a higher social class, and presents herself as having been cut adrift from her lower-middle-class roots, and of being a kind of class 'traitor' to her parents. Writing, as the epigraph to *La Place* taken from Genet suggests, is put forward as a means of atoning for her class treachery: 'Je hasarde une explication: écrire c'est le dernier recours quand on a trahi'. But in one sense Ernaux's narrator had simply fulfilled her parents' wishes. They wanted their only daughter to succeed, both economically and academically, and thus move up the social ladder, as they had, from one class to another. Their daughter completes the process of upward migration that they began, moving from peasant stock to become *petits commerçants*. The irony of the daughter's predicament is summed up at the end of *Une femme*: 'Il fallait que ma mère, née dans un milieu dominé, dont elle a voulu sortir, devienne histoire, pour que je sente moins seule et factice dans le monde dominant des mots et des idées où, *selon son désir*, je suis passée' (*6*, p.106, my emphasis). Thus, one of the narrator's motivations for writing about her mother in *Une Femme* is the fact that, paradoxically, her fulfilment of her mother's social ambitions has led to a situation in which she has left her mother behind, and furthermore has acquired the linguistic and conceptual tools with which to condemn her as humiliatingly 'inferior'. And although the father's attitude is presented as being rather more ambiguous (the narrator of *La Place* is haunted by the thought that she sensed in her father 'la peur OU PEUT-ÊTRE LE DÉSIR que je n'y arrive pas' (*4*, p.80)), she equally stresses that his enduring hope is that his daughter 'serai[t] *mieux que lui*' (*4*, p.74). This dilemma has been described by critics as the 'double bind' (*29*) or 'l'entre-deux' (*59*) of being in-between two classes. *La Place* and *La Honte* reveal the extent to which both Ernaux and her parents suffer from their liminal socio-economic situation. The narrating daughter has gained the financial independence and social freedoms wished for by her parents, but only by learning how to speak the language of the 'enemy' in terms of economic power structures. She neither feels fully integrated in the 'classes dominantes' nor fully accepted in her parent's milieu. In fact, leaving her past behind is often characterised in Ernaux's writing as a kind of loss.

The terms frequently employed by Ernaux to describe her experiences of moving from one class to another — 'la classe dominante', 'la classe dominée', 'l'héritage' — are by no means accidental. They are taken from the work of French sociologist Pierre Bourdieu, who prefers the terms 'dominé' and 'dominant' to the Marxist categorisations of the proletariat and the bourgeoisie. As I shall discuss further, Ernaux's use of Bourdieu's terms helps her to illustrate how her parents, while having succeeded economically to some degree, were still defined by others as socially inferior. In 2002, Ernaux published an obituary for Bourdieu in *Le Monde*. In it, she describes the impact of his theories on her conception of the interrelationship between class, education and culture — the very themes she was keen to broach in her writing after her father's death. Reading Bourdieu's work, Ernaux writes, compelled her to question everything that she had once taken for granted: 'l'être qu'on croyait être n'est plus le même, la vision qu'on avait de soi et des autres dans la société se déchire, notre place, nos goûts, rien n'est plus naturel, allant de soi dans le fonctionnement des choses apparemment les plus ordinaires de la vie' (*20*, p.16). While Ernaux's quest for suitable literary models when she first set about writing the story of her father's life and their relationship had been fruitless, the sociological studies published by Bourdieu provided her with the impetus to write and, crucially, with an intellectual framework with which to elucidate and universalise her personal experiences:

> Ce que j'avais à dire — pour aller vite, le passage du monde dominé au monde dominant, par les études — , je ne l'avais jamais vu exprimé comme je le sentais. Et un livre m'autorisait, en quelque sorte, à entreprendre cette mise au jour. Un livre me poussait comme aucun texte dit littéraire ne l'avait fait, à oser affronter cette "histoire", ce livre, c'était *Les Héritiers* de Bourdieu et Passeron. (*21*, p.87)

The importance of Bourdieu's concepts in Ernaux's writing cannot be overemphasised, and this is particularly true in relation to *La Place* and *La Honte*. In this chapter, I shall outline some of Bourdieu's key ideas about class, education and culture before going on to show how they are introduced into and endorsed by Ernaux's texts.

Bourdieu's model of society and social relations has its roots in Marxist theories of class and conflict. He defines any society, or what he terms a social 'field', as the site of a struggle for power between 'les classes dominantes' and 'les classes dominées'. The goal of all social groups is to gain 'legitimacy' through the amassing of capital, which will thus ensure the continuing dominance of their social group. By capital, however, Bourdieu does not just mean economic capital (as is the case with most Marxist theories). Rather, capital is extended to cover any material and symbolic goods that present themselves as worthy of being sought after within a particular social formation. In other words, Bourdieu argues that it is not only money or property that is used by individuals or institutions to gain dominance within a society, and thus to reproduce themselves over time. The amassing of what Bourdieu terms 'cultural capital' — the knowledge of the particular forms of behaviour, language, art, literature, music and so forth which are valued by the ruling classes — can be equally as effective. Economic capital is, of course, easily transferable from generation to generation, which makes it particularly useful in continuing the process of reproducing class legitimacy and domination over time. In order to maintain the legitimacy of different forms of cultural capital, however, institutions such as the education system have to function to prevent precisely what the 1946 Constitution claims it is designed to facilitate — that is, equal access and upward mobility for individuals from all classes. And, as I shall now discuss, this is exactly, according to Bourdieu, how the French education system works.

Bourdieu's theorisation of the relationship between class and education in France is elaborated in two texts: *Les Héritiers* (1964) and *La Reproduction* (1970). Here, he argues that although schools and universities may appear to offer the chance for children from lower social classes to enter more highly paid and high status professions, they work in fact to maintain the status quo of the ruling classes. This is because they reward the cultural capital that bourgeois students already possess, and lower-middle-class or working-class students have to work hard to acquire:

> La culture de l'élite est si proche de la culture de l'Ecole que l'enfant originaire d'un milieu petit-bourgeois (et *a fortiori* paysan ou ouvrier) ne peut acquérir que laborieusement ce qui est donné au fils de la classe cultivée, le style, le goût, l'esprit, bref, ce savoir-faire et ce savoir-vivre qui sont naturels à une classe, parce qu'ils sont la culture de cette classe. Pour les uns, l'apprentissage de la culture de l'élite est une conquête, chèrement payée; pour les autres, un héritage.[5]

In this context, Bourdieu argues that all educational practice (what he terms 'action pédagogique') is a form of symbolic violence, in that it constitutes the imposition of a 'cultural arbitrary', a set of subjective cultural values, by the 'classes dominantes'. As a result of the imposition and valorisation of this arbitrary set of values, bourgeois students find in their schooling a confirmation of the value and validity of the knowledge they already possess. In contrast, in order for students from the 'classes dominées' to succeed, they must reject their cultural backgrounds and acquire instead the cultural capital of their more privileged classmates. And, as Bourdieu comments and as Ernaux demonstrates, the acquisition of cultural capital that is alien to an individual's social background can be extremely costly in personal and psychological terms.

Ernaux's representation of the French education system in *La Place* and *La Honte* is markedly consistent with Bourdieu's theories. In fact, Ernaux's account of her experiences as an educationally successful child of lower-middle-class parents in post-

---

[5] Pierre Bourdieu et Jean-Claude Passeron, *Les Héritiers: les étudiants et la culture* (Paris: Minuit, 1964), p.41.

war France is overtly indebted to Bourdieu's arguments as they are expounded in *Les Héritiers* and *La Reproduction*. The process of education involves an acceptance of the norms of bourgeois culture and, consequently, a rejection of the cultural values acquired during her childhood, which are viewed as worthless in the context of her school and university. It is worth reiterating at this point that Ernaux's narrator receives mixed messages about what is valued during her childhood, because of the social migration undergone by her parents. While the mother attempts to eradicate any remaining traces of the 'héritage' of her peasant roots and inculcate her daughter instead with the aspirational values of the lower middle classes, her father continues to some extent to adhere to the values of the rural working classes. In both cases, however, the parents' legacy is dismissed as worthless by the bourgeois authorities to which their daughter is subject during her education. This is evident from the opening scene of *La Place*, in which the narrator sits the oral exam for the CAPES (Certificat d'aptitude professionnelle à l'enseignement secondaire). This episode reveals how she has managed to amass the cultural capital necessary to confirm her membership of an elite class: 'Une femme corrigeait des copies avec hauteur, sans hésiter. Il suffisait de franchir correctement l'heure suivante pour être autorisée à faire comme elle toute ma vie' (*4*, p.11). Once her performance has been given the stamp of approval by her bourgeois examiners, she has been accepted into the 'monde dominant des mots et des idées' that exclude and condemn her parents' tastes, habits and culture. It is poignant, from this perspective, that the passage she is given to analyse is taken from Honoré de Balzac's *Le Père Goriot*, a novel which deals with the story of a wealthy business man from humble origins, whose obsessive love for his daughters and desire that they enter the upper classes leads him eventually to impoverish and humiliate himself. In *Le Père Goriot*, the upper-class daughters, ashamed of their roots, finally reject their father and he dies penniless and unloved. Thus, in *La Place*, it is ironically a legitimised interpretation of a canonical French novel about two daughters' rejection of their father through shame at his social origins that brings about

Ernaux's narrator's own entry into the upper echelons of society and substantiates her consequent feelings of shame about her parents' lives. The subject matter of the text she is required to teach, so relevant in relation to Ernaux's own situation, is, however, lost on the narrator of *La Place* as we are told that her sole desire at this point is to prove herself worthy of acceptance: 'Devant une classe de première, des matheux, j'ai expliqué vingt-cinq lignes — il fallait les numéroter — du *Père Goriot* de Balzac. [...] Pendant un quart d'heure, [l'inspecteur] a mélangé critiques, éloges, conseils, et j'écoutais à peine, me demandant si tout cela signifiait que j'étais reçue' (*4*, pp.11–12).

The description of the CAPES exam has strong resonances of Bourdieu's sociological observations about the nature of educational achievement in post-war France. In *Les Héritiers*, Bourdieu and Passeron include as an epigraph a quotation taken from a study by the anthropologist Margaret Mead. She describes the rites of a tribe in which accession to the ruling classes comes about by means of an authenticated 'vision' experienced by a young man. The vision, however, was only seen as authentic if it followed the norms (which were never overtly elucidated) of previous authenticated visions, and if it was verified by the ruling elite, the members of which 'knew' a true vision when they saw one: 'En principe, l'entrée dans la société était validée par une vision librement recherchée, mais le dogme selon lequel une vision était une expérience mystique non spécifiée que tout jeune homme pouvait rechercher et trouver, était contrebalancé par le secret, très soigneusement gardé, concernant tout ce qui constituait une vision véritable.'[6] Bourdieu and Passeron intend Mead's anthropological observations to function as an allegory for the inequality of access in post-war France to its prestigious institutions of higher education. It is equally possible to see a parallel case in the 'cérémonie' (*4*, p.12) of the CAPES exam sat by Ernaux's narrator which resembles, as Christian Garaud notes, 'un rite vain et dérisoire' (*40*, p.197). It is not her personal response or original insights into the text that matter, but her

---

[6] Bourdieu and Passeron, *Les Héritiers*, p.1.

successful imitation of the performance of the elite that allows her to enter a higher social order.

The CAPES exam is presented as the apex of the process of 'embourgeoisement', or the acquisition of values, tastes and modes of behaviour legitimised by the ruling classes, undergone by Ernaux's narrator. In Siobhan McIlvanney's words, it is put forward as 'the last major event which separates her from her father by ensconcing her more deeply in the bourgeoisie, a separation rendered final by his death' (*45*, pp.100–01). Indeed, the exam and her father's funeral are linked in the text both by the use of the term 'cérémonie' to describe them and by the narrator's doubts as to their relative chronology (*4*, p.13). Her position as a kind of 'traitor' to her working class roots is confirmed by the final scene of *La Place*, in which she reveals her inability to communicate with a supermarket checkout girl that she recognises as her former student (*4*, pp.112–13). As Tony McNeill notes: 'The narrator is unable to remember why she had been sent to technical school nor what stream she was put in. […] [She] has become an accomplice in a system which perpetuates social divisions and inequalities. She has made it but does nothing to help those who are disadvantaged within the school system' (*47*, p.2). This powerful closing scene, though, is more ambiguous in its message than this initial analysis would suggest. It indicates the arbitrary nature of educational success, and leaves the future fate of the former student deliberately uncertain. Thus, although Ernaux is, in one sense, on the other side of the dividing line in terms of class hierarchies, the checkout girl also acts as a double for her younger self. From this perspective, she is not only a failed student that the narrator-teacher is unable or unwilling to help, but also embodies an alternative fate that was potentially in store for the narrator, as the latter could easily have followed in her parents' footsteps and worked in a shop. The final image, of the girl mechanically moving grocery items from left to right, can be read as a metaphor for the lack of agency frequently experienced by individuals when faced with the capricious machinations of a system in which the odds are stacked against them. The text thus ends on a flat and depressing note, suggesting that inequalities will never be overcome when a system functions according to the acquisition of an arbitrary set of cultural values rather than a truly egalitarian principle.

The process of 'embourgeoisement' for Ernaux's narrator begins at an early age, at her Catholic 'école privée', a fact that is made particularly clear in *La Honte*. Her attendance at the private Catholic girls' school reveals the aspirational motivations of her lower-middle-class parents, who have had to make economic sacrifices in order to afford it. Yet ironically its teachings lead to a sense of alienation between daughter and parents, as she learns to reject their habits and lives. *La Honte* shows how as a schoolgirl Ernaux's narrator was imbued with specific kinds of cultural values, and that these values were closely aligned not only with the middle classes but equally with Catholicism. In her school, the pupils were taught by nuns or by single middle-class women, who imparted a vision of the world that combined bourgeois propriety with religious piety. Life at the school was thus dominated by specifically Catholic language, beliefs, rituals and symbolism. Within this context or 'social field', the acquisition of legitimised cultural capital, and consequent rejection of other cultures and habits, operated in several different spheres. It concerned, for instance, the demarcation of the kinds of books, films, music, art and so on that were considered to be suitable and those which were considered to be unsuitable:

> Tout ce qui renforce ce monde est encouragé, tout ce qui le menace est dénoncé et vilipendé. Il est bien vu:
> [...] d'avoir toujours un chapelet dans la poche
> d'acheter *Ames vaillantes*
> de posséder le Missel vespéral romain de Dom Lefebvre
> [...]
> Il est mal vu:
> d'apporter en classe des livres et des journaux autres que des ouvrages religieux et *Ames vaillantes*. [...]
> d'aller au cinéma en dehors des séances scolaires (*Jeanne d'Arc, Monsieur Vincent, Le curé d'Ars*). (*11*, pp.88–90)

Exposure to non-legitimised books, films and images was strictly controlled. While for some pupils this segregation of 'good' and 'bad' literature and cinema might not conflict with their parents' views, for children from different backgrounds it was a source of tension and confusion. In *La Place* and *La Honte*, the narrator's mother is seen to approve of the school and attempts, at least initially, to collude in her daughter's 'embourgeoisement': 'elle a poursuivi son désir d'apprendre à travers moi. Le soir, à table, elle me faisait parler de mon école. Elle lisait les livres que je lisais, conseillés par le libraire' (*6*, pp.57–58). As a practising Catholic, she equally shores up the school's value system by providing her daughter with 'legitimate' reading material:

> Les journaux et les romans qu'elle me donne à lire, en plus de la *Bibliothèque verte*, ne vont pas à l'encontre des préceptes de l'école privée. Ils obéissent tous à la condition sans laquelle il n'est pas de lecture autorisée, *pouvoir être mis entre toutes les mains* donc *Les Veillées des chaumières*, *Le Petit Echo de la mode*, les romans de Delly et de Max du Veuzit. Sur la couverture de certains livres figure le label *Ouvrage couronné par l'Académie française*, attestant leur conformité aux exigences de la morale autant et sinon plus que leur intérêt littéraire. (*11*, p.111)

While at this stage the narrator's mother confirms the value of and even increases her daughter's stock of cultural capital, the father's behaviour and cultural tastes are antithetical to those approved by the school and the church. Irritated by his wife's adherence to Catholicism (*11*, pp.113–14), her father also makes little attempt to follow his daughter in her studies, and feels distanced from her school, which seems to belong to a different world: 'L'école, une institution religieuse voulue par ma mère, était pour lui un univers terrible qui, comme l'île de Laputa dans *Les Voyages de Gulliver*, flottait au-dessus de moi pour diriger mes manières, tous mes gestes' (*4*, p.73).

The extent to which the narrator's father feels alienated from the daughter's Catholic school, and oscillates between pride and alarm in relation to her gradual accretion of cultural capital, is related in *La Place* to his own education. In the same way as Ernaux benefited from post-war educational reforms, her father's education was a result of the Ferry reforms of the 1880s, which aimed to make secular primary education free and compulsory for the masses. In *La Place*, the father's teacher attempts to impose order, discipline and hygiene on his peasant pupils, and is angry when the father has to miss classes to help with the harvest (*4*, p.29). In this sense, the teacher attempts to give his pupils the possibility of having a better life than their families, not wishing them to be 'misérables comme eux' (*4*, p.29). Yet, French schoolchildren in the early part of the twentieth century were equally educated to accept their place in life, and to develop a patriotic love of their country and a sense of their duties as law-abiding French citizens. The only book Ernaux's father remembers from his own education, we are told in *La Place*, is *Le Tour de France par deux enfants*. This is an early school textbook that tells the story of two orphans from Lorraine who travel around France to meet their uncle in Marseille. It is thus a portrait of France from the perspective of 'outsiders' (Alsace Lorraine was German territory from 1871 to 1918), and praises France and the Republican values it is made to embody. The book paints a picture not of a divided or revolutionary nation, but of one that does not suffer from regional discontent because the country is united by the same universal noble sentiments and is peopled by contented inhabitants. In a recent essay, Ernaux tellingly describes the textbook, that she defines as the 'bible du parfait citoyen de la Troisième République', in the following terms: 'Un livre qui martelait à toutes les pages la valeur du travail en ignorant soigneusement le mot grève, faisait des riches et des pauvres des catégories naturelles et immuables, assignait à chacun sa place' (*18*, p.47). Included in *La Place* are various platitudes taken from the book: 'Apprendre à toujours être heureux de notre sort'; 'Une famille unie par l'affection possède la meilleure des richesses'; 'L'homme actif ne perd pas une minute, et, à la fin de la journée, il se trouve que chaque heure lui a apporté quelque chose' (*4*, pp.30–31). Ernaux's narrator goes on to imply that her father has lived by this creed; that, in other words, he has partly based his identity on the ideology he absorbed from this textbook, designed to promote a patriotic love of France and the Third Republic and to accept one's place in the 'natural order of things'. His constant fear of feeling 'out of place' — 'la peur d'être déplacé' (*4*, p.59) — is connected in *La Place* to the discourse to which he was exposed during his schooldays. He has accepted his role and feels uncomfortable in relation to 'high' culture, which he feels is out of his sphere. This is made particularly clear in the scene in *La Place* when he takes his daughter to a library. Like the CAPES examiners with which the narrative opens, the librarians are presented as gatekeepers to the world of high culture:

> Deux hommes nous regardaient venir depuis un comptoir très haut barrant l'accès aux rayons. Mon père m'a laissé demander: "On voudrait emprunter des livres." L'un des hommes aussitôt: "Qu'est-ce que vous voulez comme livres?" A la maison, on n'avait pas pensé qu'il fallait savoir d'avance ce qu'on voulait, être capable de citer des titres aussi facilement que des marques de biscuits. On a choisi à notre place, *Colomba* pour moi, un roman *léger* de Maupassant pour mon père. (*4*, pp.111–12)

The father's inability to interact with the librarians is indicated by the use of a child's perspective (they both appear to gaze upwards towards the high counter) and the father's silence. Unlike the narrator when she sits the CAPES exam, the father is marked as not belonging. He is not given access 'aux rayons', and is given a 'light' novel to read, confirming his lowly status. Even in this early scene it is the daughter who attempts, albeit unsuccessfully, to communicate with the adjudicators of what counts as cultural capital. And, as the narrative development of *La Place* makes clear, the daughter's acquisition of cultural capital, firstly at her Catholic school, and then at university (where different kinds of cultural capital, such as, somewhat paradoxically, a knowledge of the in-vogue anti-establishment writers and thinkers, are legitimised), gradually increases the distance between father and daughter. Eventually they find themselves on opposing sides of the 'comptoir', that is, the dividing line between the 'invalid' culture of the 'classes dominées' and the 'valid' culture of the 'classes dominantes'.

It is not only cultural tastes, however, that are seen to endow an individual with a 'place' within the ruling classes. It is equally, in broader terms, the modes of behaviour, the way an individual speaks, dresses, eats and deals with his or her bodily functions that marks him or her out as a member of a particular class. This is what Bourdieu defines as 'habitus', an individual's beliefs and dispositions. Bourdieu's concept of habitus suggests that individuals do not have totally free choice in the ways they behave and react. Rather, according to their particular social group, they are predisposed to behave in certain ways and to have a certain picture of the world. These dispositions and practices exist largely in the realm of the unconscious and include things such as body movements and postures, as well as opinions and knowledge about the world. In her Catholic girls' school, Ernaux's narrator learns to reject her father's 'habitus' in favour of new modes of behaviour and ways of thinking. The school's role, in Ernaux's texts, is to regulate and modify its pupils' behaviour as much as it is to pass on legitimised knowledge about particular academic subjects. There are numerous examples of the narrator correcting modes of speech and behaviour that she has learnt at home. After having outlined her father's pleasure in spitting and sneezing in the yard, for example, the narrator of *La Place* shows how her schoolteacher disapproves of such behaviour and admonishes a pupil for sneezing in the classroom (*4*, p.69). Likewise, the ways of speaking and expressing (or not expressing) emotions she has learnt at home frequently come into conflict, as I shall discuss in more detail in the next chapter, with those of others encountered at school or church (*4*, pp.71–72). As she grows older, the narrator begins to criticise everything her father does, from the way he washes lettuces (*4*, p.81) to his eating habits (*4*, p.82) and his political ideas (*4*, p.83). At these points in the narrative, the daughter embodies the gaze of the ruling classes, inspecting her father's 'habitus' and finding it wanting.

Moreover, if the mother's cultural tastes concur, at least to some extent, with those authenticated by the school and church, her behaviour and habits, like those of her husband, do not. This is made evident in both texts. In *La Honte*, for example, Ernaux's narrator states: 'Tout de notre existence est devenu signe de honte. La pissotière dans la cour, la chambre commune — où, selon une habitude répandue dans notre milieu et due au manque d'espace, je dormais avec mes parents —, les gifles et les gros mots, de ma mère, les clients ivres et les familles qui achetaient à crédit (*11*, p.139). One of the most difficult scenes to read in *La Honte* concerns the sight of the narrator's mother as the former returns with her school-friends and teacher from a school trip:

> Ma mère est apparue dans la lumière de la porte, hirsute, muette de sommeil, dans une chemise de nuit froissée et tachée (on s'essuyait avec, après avoir uriné). Mlle L. et les élèves, deux ou trois, se sont arrêtées de parler. Ma mère a bredouillé un bonsoir auquel personne n'a répondu. Je me suis engouffrée dans l'épicerie pour faire cesser la scène. Je venais de voir pour la première fois ma mère avec le regard de l'école privée. (*11*, p.117)

As Loraine Day notes, this scene reveals the narrator's mother to be at odds with the ideas about seemly behaviour put forward by her school: 'Her [mother's] undisciplined, shapeless form is at once in excess and in deficit in relation to the middle-class femininity of the maternal image which has currency at the narrator's school' (*33*, p.157). The young girl here takes on the gaze of the bourgeoisie, sharing the horror of her teacher and school-friends in relation to her mother's all-too-obvious failure to fit into bourgeois norms of social and bodily behaviour, or what Bourdieu terms 'habitus'. This episode effectively illustrates the extent to which shame about one's social origins is not only related to the books an individual reads (or does not read), to his or her cultural habits and knowledge, but also relates to the relationship individuals have with their bodies.

Yet *La Place* and *La Honte* do not only describe the narrator's rejection of her parents' shameful lack of 'cultural capital' in relation to the bourgeois norms with which she is indoctrinated at school, church and university. In several key episodes in both texts, the narrator also makes a plea for the value of the cultural 'heritage' that she is forced to leave behind, a legacy that is particularly associated with her father. In this sense there is an important distinction to be made between the gaze of the young girl the narrator once was, critical and full of shame, and that of the adult writer, who wishes to distance herself from her 'shameful' past behaviour in relation to her parents. In the scene in *La Honte* quoted above, for example, the adult narrator does not fully share the horrified gaze of the adolescent as she is faced with her mother's 'undisciplined' body. Rather, as Day suggests, 'the narrator is in a very ambiguous and invidious position. Because she identifies with her mother, she feels included in the critical gaze directed at the older woman; at the same time, however, she is the subject or agent of the gaze, she sees her mother with the critical eye of the outsider' (*33*, p.157). The perspective of the narrator oscillates between identification with her younger self (who is learning to share the critical gaze of the ruling classes), and identification with her mother, and her mother's class-rooted 'failings' as marked on/by her body and soiled clothing. As a class migrant, the narrator still has one foot in each camp, and the oscillation between competing perspectives in this way, as I suggested in Chapter 2, enables Ernaux to express her narrator's split identity. Thus, whilst making clear the difficulties faced by the educated daughter in relation to her parents, the narrators of *La Place* and *La Honte* also emphasise the fact that writing — so often the source of denigration and disempowerment of the lower classes — can equally be a means of re-valuing non-bourgeois culture and identity.

More specifically, in the second half of *La Place* Ernaux's narrator is particularly keen to stress that her father was not as 'uncultured' as her education had led her to believe, and often positively contrasts his cultural activities, that bear witness to his working-class roots, with her newly acquired bourgeois cultural values:

> Toujours prêt à m'emmener au cirque, aux films *bêtes*, au feu d'artifice. A la foire, on montait dans le train fantôme, l'Himalaya, on entrait voir la femme la plus grosse du monde et le Lilliputien. Il n'a jamais mis les pieds dans un musée. Il s'arrêtait devant un beau jardin, des arbres en fleur, une ruche, regardait les filles bien en chair. Il admirait les constructions immenses, les grands travaux modernes (le pont de Tancarville). Il aimait la musique de cirque, les promenades en voiture dans la campagne [...]. (*4*, p.65)

She is equally quick to suggest that he had knowledge and skills — about, for example, bird-calls, gardening and weather prediction (*4*, pp.67–68) — but it was knowledge that was not valued either in her private school nor in the urban, petty-bourgeois class into which he had moved with his wife: 'Personne à Y..., dans les classes moyennes, commerçants du centre, employés de bureau, ne veut avoir l'air de "sortir de sa campagne". Faire paysan signifie qu'on n'est pas évolué, toujours en retard sur ce qui se fait, en vêtements, langage, allure' (*4*, p.70). The tragedy of the father's position in *La Place* is that his own liminal status in terms of social class means that he too comes to devalue his knowledge and cultural tastes — as does his wife — and is aware of his lack of cultural capital. In Bourdieu's terms, he has 'internalised' the cultural norms of the 'classes dominantes' and has, at least in part, adopted their denigratory attitudes towards his own cultural practices. The father's sense of shame is therefore further compounded by the fact that his knowledge, skills and cultural habits are not recognised as having any worth or value in his daughter's school, which is made only too evident in his daughter's rejection of the knowledge and cultural experiences he has to offer her: 'Je pensais qu'il ne pouvait plus rien pour moi. Ses mots et ses idées n'avaient pas cours dans les salles de français ou de philo, les séjours à canapé de velours rouge des amies de classe' (*4*, p.83). A later awareness as an adult of the pain such a rejection must have caused her father is tentatively put forward as one of the narrator's motivations for writing the book. *La Place* is to some extent a peace offering to her father that, the narrator hopes, will redress the adolescent's short-sightedness in refusing to share any linguistic, intellectual or cultural common ground with her father: 'J'écris peut-être parce qu'on n'avait plus rien à se dire' (*4*, p.84).

Recording her parents' 'habitus', then, is at once for Ernaux a public political statement and a private act of atonement. On the one hand, she confirms Bourdieu's findings about the effects of education on the children of lower-middle or working-class parents. From this perspective, *La Place* and *La Honte* can be read, to a large extent, as case studies alongside Bourdieu's sociological publications, especially *Les Héritiers* and *La Reproduction*. On the other, Ernaux's literary works are a personal means of assuaging her own guilt for her collusion in her parents' exclusion from 'le monde dominant des mots et des idées'. By endowing them with 'literary' identities she grants them a 'place' in this world, and at the same time asserts the value of the 'héritage' that her education had forced her to leave behind.

4. Language and style

That Ernaux's writing incorporates an interrogation of the uses and abuses of language is signalled by the epigraph to *La Honte*, which is taken from Paul Auster's *The Invention of Solitude*: 'Language is not truth. It is the way we exist in the world'. In Ernaux's work, as the above quotation implies, language, the only means we have at our disposal to decipher, interact with and perhaps transcend the limitations of the world around us, is also not to be fully trusted. Words are not a set of dependable tools with clearly defined and immutable meanings to manipulate at will in order straightforwardly to convey the truth. Rather, individuals are shown to be as much the products as the producers of language. In Ernaux's texts, people are judged, betrayed and, at least to some extent, constructed by the language they use. In *La Honte*, for instance, the narrator points to the centrality of language in the process of identity construction, commenting that one of her achieved aims has been to identify 'les langages qui me traversaient et constituaient ma perception de moi-même et du monde' (*11*, p.115). Further, linguistic differences, as much as economic differences, are consistently represented in Ernaux's writing as constituting one of the most persistent markers of class. As a result, language is a constant source of anxiety and tension for the narrator's family: 'Tout ce qui touche au langage est dans mon souvenir motif de rancœur et de chicanes douloureuses, bien plus que l'argent' (*4*, p.64). Yet, despite the way in which individuals can be entrapped by language into a particular way of speaking, thinking and behaving (and one that can be condemned by others as inferior), language is all we have to make sense of the world in which we live. Language is thus not rejected or refused by Ernaux — retreating into silence, as the episode with the father in the library at the end of *La Place* illustrates, leads to disempowerment

and defeat. On the contrary, she attempts, through her production of
literary texts, to use language as a kind of bridge between her
present and past selves, enabling her narrators to atone publicly for
their 'class treachery', and at the same time to come to terms on a
personal level with their grief (*La Place*) or trauma (*La Honte*). As
Lyn Thomas argues, Ernaux's texts allow us to see language as both
imprisoning and liberating in terms of our individual and collective
identities: 'On the one hand, words seem heavy, pregnant with
meaning, conveying a culture which contains, but at times stifles;
on the other hand, they are light and airy, the vehicles of a freedom
which [...] is almost frightening' (*58*, p.85). In this chapter, I shall
examine firstly the ways in which Ernaux's texts reveal how words
can be 'stifling' markers of class. Secondly, I shall explore the
linguistic strategies put into place by Ernaux's narrators in an
attempt to avoid the pitfalls of class-ridden language. Finally, I shall
discuss some of the implications of the distinctive stylistic features
adopted by Ernaux since the publication of *La Place*, focusing in
particular on the ways in which the style and structure of her
literary texts flag up the complexity and, ultimately, the inseparable
nature of the interwoven strands that make up an individual's
identity.

In both *La Place* and *La Honte*, Ernaux's narrators make a
clear distinction between the bourgeois language encountered at
school and university and the language used in the family home. As
a fellow class migrant, the daughter faces a similar problem to her
father, in that she gradually ceases to speak the language spoken by
her parents. Her parents are ashamed of the fact that her
grandfather was illiterate: 'Chaque fois qu'on m'a parlé de [mon
grand-père], cela commençait par "il ne savait ni lire ni écrire",
comme si sa vie et son caractère ne se comprenaient pas sans cette
donnée initiale' (*4*, p.26). In contrast, her father 'a réussi à savoir
lire et écrire sans faute' (*4*, p.29), and is proud of the fact that he no
longer speaks the patois spoken by his parents: 'Pour mon père, le
patois était quelque chose de vieux et de laid, un signe d'infériorité.
Il était fier d'avoir pu s'en débarrasser en partie' (*4*, p.62). Yet,
although he has surpassed his father in terms of the social mobility

afforded by the ability to read and write standard French, he remains aware of other linguistic failings. In one scene in *La Place*, for example, the father is overcome with shame when he misinterprets a solicitor's instruction to write 'lu et approuvé' on a document and writes instead 'à prouver': 'Gêne, obsession de cette faute, sur la route du retour. L'ombre de l'indignité' (*4*, p.59). Similarly, he is distressed by being unable to understand what the headmistress means by a 'costume de ville' in which his daughter is supposed to be dressed, as he risks exposing his family's social 'inferiority' by misinterpreting the expression (*4*, p.60). These 'errors' are increasingly evident to his daughter, who quickly becomes aware of the gap that exists between her parents' linguistic habits and the language she is taught to use at school: 'Puisque la maîtresse me "reprenait", plus tard j'ai voulu reprendre mon père, lui annoncer que "se parterrer" ou "quart moins d'onze heures" n'*existaient pas*' (*4*, p.64). It is not a case of accepting the dissimilarities between the words, expressions and grammar employed by different language-users in the daughter's environment as so many harmless linguistic variations. There is a clear hierarchy put in place by her educators that leads her to refuse to acknowledge the validity of forms and expressions used by her father that have not been given the stamp of approval at her school.

Language becomes a weapon in class warfare, and the daughter learns how to belittle her father by using the damning language of the bourgeoisie, labelling him as a member of 'la catégorie des *gens simples* ou *modestes* ou *braves gens*' (*4*, p.80). The use of such expressions reveals the extent to which as an adolescent she has absorbed and accepted a bourgeois worldview. As Christine Fau remarks, 'elle s'est détachée de ses parents au point d'emprunter les définitions des autres pour parler d'eux froidement' (*36*, p.507). Although such definitions may appear to be neutral, the narrator shows them to be based on a bourgeois understanding of the inferiority of the masses, and whose function is to mask the economic differences that lie beneath them. They stand in stark contrast to Ernaux's preferred terms — 'la classe dominante' and 'la classe dominée' — that she takes from the work of Pierre Bourdieu (and that I discuss in detail in Chapter 3).

As an adolescent, in sum, Ernaux's narrator uses the language she learns at school to belittle and condemn her parents as linguistically, socially and culturally inferior. When writing as an adult looking back on her past, Ernaux's narrator is again using language as a weapon in class warfare, but unlike the adolescent she once was, this time she is on the side of her parents. Ernaux states in *L'Ecriture comme un couteau* that she produces in her texts 'une narratrice [...] qui écrit dans "la langue de l'ennemi", qui utilise le savoir-écrire "volé" aux dominants' (*21*, p.33). In a manner reminiscent of Shakespeare's Caliban, who in *The Tempest* bitterly retorts to his teacher Prospero that 'You taught me language, and my profit on't / Is I know how to curse. The red plague on you / For learning me your language', Ernaux's narrators 'steal' the language of the 'classes dominantes' in order to use it to denounce them as 'the enemy'.[7] Ernaux's narrator exploits the skill with words she has developed as a result of her education in order to expose the socio-economic hierarchy that underpins linguistic variation, and in so doing attempts to reintegrate and revalorise the language of the 'classes dominées' to which she once belonged.

Ernaux's works reveal, moreover, that it is not only the lexicon that counts in mastering the language of the ruling classes. Tone and register are equally significant linguistic markers of class difference. In the parents' milieu, for example, politeness is reserved for strangers and for those who are considered to be socially superior, and is not the norm in everyday exchanges between friends and family: 'Barrière de protection, la politesse était inutile entre mari et femme, parents et enfants, ressentie même comme de l'hypocrisie ou de la méchanceté. La rudesse, la hargne et la criaillerie constituaient les formes normales de la communication familiale' (*11*, p.70). It comes as a shock to discover that this is not the case in all households: 'La politesse entre parents et enfants m'est demeurée longtemps un mystère' (*4*, p.72). Further, in the childhood world of Ernaux's narrators, words are used for

---

[7] William Shakespeare, *The Tempest*, Act I, Scene 2, lines 366–68.

communicating concrete rather than abstract concepts, such as emotions (*11*, p.74). Modes of expression such as metaphor (*4*, p.46) and irony likewise remain 'unknown' to the narrators' parents (*4*, pp.46, 65). In contrast, the daughter, increasingly absorbing the bourgeois credo of her school and peers, begins to adopt not only a different vocabulary, but also a different tone: 'On mangeait sans parler. [...] Je faisais de "l'ironie" [...]. Je lisais la "vraie" littéra-ture, et je recopiais des phrases, des vers, qui, je croyais, exprimaient mon "âme", l'indicible de ma vie' (*4*, p.79). In favouring irony and soaking up poetic language that evokes abstract concepts through literary techniques such as metaphor, she is adopting modes of expression that are far removed from the linguistic habits of her parents. Christian Roche summarises: 'Les codes du monde bourgeois, que [la narratrice de *La Place*] utilise désormais, appartiennent au domaine de l'artifice, où les mots sont déviés de leur sens "naturel" notamment au moyen de l'ironie. La langue devient un jeu, un ornement' (*53*, p.134). As adolescents, Ernaux's narrators espouse an ironic or poetic mode of discourse and reject that of their parents' milieu. The consequence of her adoption of these new modes of discourse, alien to her parents, is that language becomes, in Michèle Bacholle's words, 'une source — et le reflet — de l'éloignement de l'auteur vis-à-vis de ses parents' (*29*, p.39). The adolescent daughter ceases to communicate with her parents — ceases, in effect, to speak 'their' language — hence the family meals eaten in silence. Ernaux's choice as an adult author to write in a different 'literary' style to the one with which she was inculcated as an adolescent is in consequence a means of re-integrating her parents into her world.

As a result of moving from one class to another, both parents and daughter are obliged to develop a kind of bilingualism in their use of language. The parents, having themselves moved between two different socio-economic groups, have two different languages and modes of expression, one for friends and family and another for clients and strangers. Likewise, although as an adolescent the daughter rejects the language of her parents, as an adult the narrator is able to empathise both with the 'educated' language she acquired during her studies and has used since in her profession, and with the familiar words and expressions of her childhood that remain heavily charged with meaning for her. There are constant references in Ernaux's writing to the power of certain phrases that has not diminished with the passage of time. In *La Honte*, the narrator emphasises the way in which evoking the words of her childhood inexorably leads her to re-enter the world they once signified:

> Les mots que je retrouve sont opaques, des pierres impossibles à bouger. Dépourvus d'image précise. Dépourvus de sens même, celui que pourrait me fournir un dictionnaire. Sans transcendance ni rêve autour: comme de la matière. Des mots d'usage indissoluble-ment unis aux choses et aux gens de mon enfance, que je ne peux pas faire jouer. Des tables de la loi. (*11*, p.73)

Their very familiarity means that such words cannot be detached from the context in which they were originally articulated, and they thus have the power to suck the narrator back into the narrow confines of a world she no longer inhabits. Ernaux's texts do not only aim, then, to expose the extent to which language can be a key marker of class, a source of anxiety and humiliation for those who are deemed to be inferior for not employing it correctly. They are also concerned with language as a structuring element of individual and collective identities. Words have the power to conserve traces of the past, to evoke a lost world. Warren Johnson describes the archive of the language forms that Ernaux attempts to resuscitate in *La Honte* as a kind of 'primordial "langue matérielle" [...] a language deprived of sentiment and sentimentality [...] closely tied to the specific locale in which she was nurtured' (*42*, p.310). It is this quality of language that allows Ernaux to attempt to re-enter her childhood, and to interrogate the conflicting memories and emotions that such words bring forth.

One of Ernaux's objectives is thus to re-integrate into her texts the words and idioms used by her parents and by her childhood self in order to explore their continuing resonance, but without criticising, patronising or sentimentalising such language as 'inferior'. In order to do this, she employs a number of innovative literary techniques, and steers clear of what she considers to be elements of 'bourgeois' literary style. A literary model she firmly rejects in her attempt to incorporate working-class language in her texts, for example, is that of Proust. As I noted in Chapter 1, Ernaux's narrator in *La Place* is scathing about Proust's narrator's gentle mockery of the working-class linguistic habits of his maid, Françoise. In *La Place* and *La Honte* Ernaux highlights certain non-standard phrases and expressions that she associates with her parents by placing them in italics or in speech marks. However, as the narrator of *La Place* explains, this foregrounding of the parents' linguistic habits is not in order that the narrator can share a complicit smile with the reader à la Proust:

> Naturellement, aucun bonheur d'écrire, dans cette entreprise où je me tiens au plus près des mots et des phrases entendues, les soulignant parfois par des italiques. Non pour indiquer un double sens au lecteur et lui offrir le plaisir d'une complicité, que je refuse sous toutes ses formes, nostalgie, pathétique ou dérision. Simplement parce que ces mots et ces phrases disent les limites et la couleur du monde où vécut mon père, où j'ai vécu aussi. (*4*, p.46)

The aim of the writer is not to hold up the words and expressions used in her working- class childhood for either mockery or empathy. The oscillation between the simple, direct and unadorned 'écriture plate' which forms the body of her texts, and the visceral and colourful expressions of her childhood, which remain emotionally charged for the narrator, is a strategy, on the one hand, for reconstructing 'le monde où vécut mon père', and, on the other, for articulating the linguistic and cultural bilingualism of the narrator. In including examples of different registers of language, the narrator is able to flag up the gap that existed between the 'deux mondes' in between which she oscillates. Equally, the inclusion of non-standard expressions and idioms allows Ernaux to tell the untold story of a class whose linguistic habits have been misrepresented or absent from the literary domain. The phrases are shown not only to belong to the narrator's family, but to form part of a shared linguistic community, giving Ernaux's prose a flavour of an oral history of her parent's milieu. Furthermore, the kind of expressions chosen for inclusion tend to be short and pithy, often implying a kind of stoical acceptance or sharp good sense in the face of economic or personal difficulty. In this sense, as Christian Garaud notes, such language is contrasted positively, particularly in *La Place*, with the poetic, abstract prose of bourgeois literary forms such as the novel:

> Le contraste entre la langue standard et les autres registres prend-il une connotation morale: il signifie une opposition entre une langue et un discours dominant, prétentieux, sûr de soi, facilement trompeur, et une langue et un discours dominé, humble, mais vrai. [...] La brièveté des paroles citées contribue à faire des parents des personnes réservées mais pleines de bon sens, ayant durement acquis une sorte de sagesse qui prend volontiers une forme proverbiale. (*40*, pp.209–10)

The technique of allowing the parents' voices to be heard (unembellished and untainted by the distortions of the literary techniques of bourgeois novelists) aims in part to put them forward as embodiments of the unacknowledged commendable attitudes and survival strategies of the 'classes dominées'. From this perspective, the use of italics and speech marks also gives added weight to the narrator's role as 'ethnographer'. She appears distanced from the 'subjects' of her investigation, and offers a neutral, 'sociological' transcription of particular forms of dialect or sociolect.

As I remark in Chapter 2, however, the objective neutrality of the narrator is inevitably limited, as her dual roles as daughter and ethnographer frequently exist in a state of conflict. The reintegration of the language of the lower classes is, therefore, only one function of the quoted words and expressions from her childhood that is found in Ernaux's texts. Whereas *La Place* tends to place the parents' language in a positive light, in *La Honte*, the narrator implies that the language of her past has at times more negative connotations, having functioned as a barrier to understanding. Writing such words down aims to rid them of their deeply buried, quasi-sacred meanings and connotations, to place them in the public arena where others, in the form of her readers, can uproot them and breathe new life into them. The narrator offers a fascinating meditation, in this context, on the signification of the phrase she remembers using on the fateful day in 1952 in response to her horror and distress at her father's actions: 'Tu vas me faire gagner malheur' (*11*, p.15) which, as she explains in a footnote, is an expression which in Norman dialect means 'devenir fou et malheureux pour toujours à la suite d'un effroi' and which is rendered in the English translation of *La Honte* as 'You'll breathe disaster on me'.[8] The narrator elaborates in a later section of metanarrative that other linguistic or theoretical frameworks that could potentially render the scene meaningful for her, such as psychoanalysis or psychology, do not have anything like the same impact or weight as the expression '*gagner malheur*' (*11*, pp.32–33). As a child, the use of the phrase implies that she fears the long-term consequences of her father's actions. And the extent to which the adult narrator of *La Honte* underlines the ongoing 'unwritability' of the scene, conceiving the articulation of it as 'une action interdite devant entraîner un châtiment' (*11*, p.16), suggests that the scene has continued to arouse similar fears. The father's violence has been placed by the narrator at the heart of her conception of herself not only as an 'unworthy' or shameful member of the lower classes, but equally of herself as a writer. As Nancy Miller suggests, the words 'gagner malheur' have become charged with 'magical and terrifying meaning', just as the scene itself has been transformed by the narrator into 'the origin of all that brought the

---

[8] Annie Ernaux, *Shame*, translated by Tanya Leslie (New York: Seven Stories Press, 1998), p.14.

woman to writing' (*48*, p.40). Narrating the father's attempted
murder for the first time thus involves moving beyond the
signification of the scene that is incarnated by the term 'gagner
malheur', and considering it from other perspectives. The reason
this proves so difficult for the narrator is that to deny the words
their power means facing up to her childhood fears and bringing her
father's violence back into the realm of the understandable and
explicable. 'Gagner malheur', then, is not simply another example
of working-class wisdom or stoicism. Rather, the words have, fossil-
like, functioned as the depositories of a deeply embedded reaction to
a childhood trauma. Yet defying the threat of the words by writing
the scene down and sharing it with others is not, as the narrator
explains, wholly positive:

> (Une sorte de soulagement tout à l'heure en constatant
> que je continuais d'écrire comme avant, qu'il n'était
> rien arrivé de terrible.) Même, depuis que j'ai réussi à
> faire ce récit, j'ai l'impression qu'il s'agit d'un
> événement banal, plus fréquent dans les familles que je
> ne l'avais imaginé. Peut-être que le récit, tout récit, rend
> normal n'importe quel acte, y compris le plus drama-
> tique. […] Elle [la scène] est devenue une scène pour les
> autres. (*11*, p.17)

In ridding the scene of her father's violence of its talisman-like
quality, embodied in the phrase 'gagner malheur', the narrator
metamorphoses it into just another example of domestic violence.
This makes it banal, no longer a site of deep personal significance,
but a mere 'fait divers' to be casually consumed by others.
Nevertheless, the production of the written account of the scene of
her father's violence also allows her to consider the event, her
response, and her familial relationships using a different optic and
different words. In consequence, the narrator is able, at least
potentially, to absolve herself of the sense of guilt and social shame
that the scene has provoked. (I shall focus in more depth on the
dynamics of shame, guilt and writing in Chapter 5).

Ernaux's texts are not, of course, simply collages of italicised or quoted words and expressions remembered from her childhood. The body of the texts is written in standard French, but in a style that is highly distinctive. Ernaux's style stands in stark contrast to a novelist like Proust, whose extended metaphors, complex sentence structures, erudite vocabulary and subtle irony as he explores the vagaries of time, memory and identity is for Ernaux just the kind of literary style that is in essence bourgeois. Marie-France Savéan notes in this context that 'on dénombre peu de métaphores filées, pas de phrases complexes et raffinées qui, comme chez Proust, exploreraient les méandres de la mémoire' (*53*, p.91). Ernaux's rejection of a novelistic or mannered approach leads her to adopt, from *La Place* onwards, an economical, unadorned narrative style, free from long or complex sentence structures, metaphors or other rhetorical flourishes, which she terms 'écriture plate' and which she claims is the style she adopted when writing letters to her parents (*4*, p.24). As Claire-Lise Tondeur comments, her adoption of such a style is a deliberate political strategy on her part, closely linked to her desire for authenticity in her depiction of her parents' existence: 'Pour elle, l'écriture plate n'est pas une notion péjorative mais au contraire un rejet du pittoresque, du trucage artistique, de l'idéalisation que pratique une certaine littérature populiste ou du pathétique cher au naturalisme' (*60*, p.145). Ernaux's texts are composed of simple vocabulary, nominal phrases and less formal tenses (the *passé composé* is preferred, for example, to the *passé simple*). Syntax is pared down to its most basic level, a fact that not only makes the texts a popular choice for non-francophone students of French literature, but which also, particularly in *La Place*, lends it a deceptive air of frankness and thoroughness, as if all angles have been considered. Clarity is a major concern, and brackets and footnotes are frequently used as a means of further elucidating any ambiguity. One of the only 'literary' devices employed by Ernaux's narrators is, as Annie Olivier points out, that of understatement: 'la litote est une des rares figures de style que l'écrivain se permette, sans doute parce qu'elle consiste à dire le moins pour suggérer le plus' (*51*, p.405). Understatement is desirable because, like 'écriture plate', it is a paring down of language to its basics, getting rid of its frills and flourishes in order to avoid the risks of sentimentality, wishful thinking, falsification or vagueness in her account of her childhood and her parents' lives. Similarly, Ernaux's frequent use of lists, especially evident in *La Honte* (*11*, pp.27–30, 58–60, 62–63, 72, 79–80, 88–91, 109–10) also has the goal of reducing language to its most basic components and thus increasing the 'objectivity' of the account. Siobhan McIlvanney points out in her discussion of Ernaux's style that 'the inclusion of [...] lists, which frequently contain sociological indicators, enables the narrator to restrict the subjective vagaries of memory by presenting information in a series of self-contained vignettes with little or no narratorial comment' (*45*, p.91). Thanks to the deployment of narrative devices such as understatement and lists, in other words, the narrator successfully presents herself as a neutral recorder of the 'signes objectifs d'une existence' (*4*, p.24), rather than as a patronising novelist or sentimental biographer.

Yet it is important to recognise that despite the anti-novelistic style of Ernaux's texts they remain in the final analysis highly constructed works of literature. In an interesting expression in *Une femme*, Ernaux claims that she wishes to locate her writing 'au-dessous de la littérature' (*6*, p.23), in some kind of neutral no man's land, 'beneath' the speciousness and deceptiveness of bourgeois literary language, but nevertheless within the sphere of 'literature'. She is proposing, in other words, a form of anti-literature in order to carve out for herself a place within the literary domain. From this perspective, her strategic choice to write in her trademark 'écriture plate' is no more 'natural' or 'authentic' than any other style. Warren Motte is careful to remind us that while 'the contract she offers to her reader in *La Place* guarantees a direct literary experience unmediated by figure or flourish', the nature of language and subjectivity render it impossible to write 'neutrally': 'This anti-mannerist stance is in itself a "manner" just as the renunciation of rhetoric constitutes a new kind of rhetoric' (*50*, p.57). And just as Ernaux's style is a carefully chosen artifice that aims to fulfil her political and personal goals, so the structure of her texts functions to give added significance to their subject-matter. The order in which events are juxtaposed, for instance, is carefully and deliberately chosen. Events, descriptions or metatextual meditations are often placed side by side in order to encourage the reader to make connections between past and present, or between the narrator's life and that of her parents. The importance of juxtaposition can by illustrated by a discussion of the final pages of *La Place*. The ending of *La Place* is composed of six brief paragraphs, each separated by spaces of varying lengths. The first three paragraphs are concerned with memories of her father. We are told that he used to take his daughter to school on his bicycle, that he was proud that she had entered the world 'qui l'avait dédaigné' (*4*, p.112), and that he used to sing a song entitled 'C'est l'aviron qui nous mène en rond'. The narrator then switches to the voice of the present, informing us that she was disappointed on reading a text entitled *L'Expérience des limites* to discover it was about metaphysics and literature. In the following paragraph, we are told that while composing *La Place* she was also marking homework and correcting student essays. The juxtaposition of these apparently disparate incidents encourages the reader to make certain connections between them, and as a result to draw certain conclusions about the message of *La Place* as a whole. We are, for instance, given an impression of circularity, implied by the title of the father's song. This is echoed in the fact that the narrative itself seems to have come full circle as father and daughter mirror each other in their roles and behaviour. Just as the father was a 'passeur entre deux rives' (*4*, p.112), so his daughter oscillates between two worlds, feeling alienated from the world of metaphysics and literature, while working in an elite profession as a teacher. The juxtaposition of these different elements in the text suggests that the daughter-narrator has succeeded in building a bridge, via her act of writing, between her identity and that of her father. She recognises their dual status as class migrants, and therefore ceases to see them as detached and separate entities, divided by class differences.

Another significant structural feature of Ernaux's writing concerns the separation of the narrative from the metatext by the

insertion of spaces on the page. These 'blancs' in the text imply
that, contrary to the desire for clarity and ethnographic objectivity,
Ernaux's project has its limitations, their existence suggesting that
there are certain elements of her past and her relationships that have
not been recounted. The spaces also break up the flow of the
narrative, which lends it a disconcerting and disjointed air. The
spaces thus underline, as Christian Roche notes, the inevitable gaps
in memory and experience which cannot be adequately captured
within the limits of a single written text: 'Les blancs qui vont
parsemer […] le texte, le découper en fragments rappelleront
constamment cette fragilité de la mémoire, ce vide qui hante le
déroulement du récit' (*53*, p.139). The spaces separating the
different sections of the text undermine the author's avowed motives
of transcription, elucidation and reconciliation. While certain
techniques, such as the juxtaposition of different episodes that I
discuss above, imply a desire to make connections and draw
parallels — between past and present, child and parent, individual
and wider social group — the 'blancs' foreground ellipses that
isolate the individual elements in time and memory. In the ending
of *La Place* that I analyse above, for example, nothing falls perfectly
into shape. The inclusion of the supermarket scene at the very end
of the text instills a sense of the indifference of economic structures
and the fragility of an individual's choices. It undercuts the
narrator's potential success as a writer able to defeat the patterns of
social inequality that have led to her family's feeling of being
'déplacée'. In Lyn Thomas's analysis, while the earlier paragraphs
emphasise a sense of unity with her father, in that she is either
physically close to him or socially categorised with him, 'the final
story cuts through these images of wholeness and solidarity' (*58*,
p.7). The inclusion of the final supermarket scene, along with the
gaps in the text that disconnect each element, leads to a sense of
dislocation and disunity, and this unsettles the reader and undermines the narrator's other apparent goal of unification and
coherence.

　　　To conclude, Ernaux's texts reveal the possibilities and
limitations of language. They use language as a weapon to expose

and condemn the domination of one social group by another, and the sense of inadequacy and humiliation this can produce. But they also suggest the inevitable failure of language to (re)capture the complexities of an individual's identity. The structure of Ernaux's texts, and particularly the gaps that separate individual sections, highlight the extent to which her narrators' goals of fully recovering and illuminating the past are ultimately unrealisable. The style and structure of *La Place* and *La Honte* frequently imply that recollection, whatever the desire for authenticity, objectivity and historical exactitude, is necessarily a collection of vivid impressions, brief flashes of sound, smell or colour rather than any kind of coherent narrative. Ernaux's narrators' hesitations about their texts' own aims and successes are an integral facet of Ernaux's writing, signalling her distrust of simplistic or idealised conclusions and her belief in the ultimate unrepresentability of the totality of the self in language.

5. Family secrets

La Place and *La Honte* both involve the revelation of family secrets. In the case of *La Place*, the narrator reveals her guilt at having assimilated the ideology of a dominant social group that refused to see any value in the lives and experiences of her parents. As the epigraph taken from Genet intimates ('Je hasarde une explication: écrire c'est le dernier recours quand on a trahi'), the narrator of *La Place* is confessing to having 'betrayed' her parents, and writing is consequently set up as a form of atonement for her past misdemeanour. In *La Honte*, Ernaux's narrator reveals the secret of her father's violence, and the traumatic ongoing effect it had on her conception of self. The 'scène' with which the narrator opens the narrative has attained iconic status, starkly separating the narrator's childhood into a 'before' and 'after' of innocence and a 'fall' into sin and shame: 'C'était le 15 juin 52. La première date précise et sûre de mon enfance. Avant, il n'y a qu'un glissement des jours et des dates inscrites au tableau et sur les cahiers' (*11*, p.16). In Ernaux's writing, exposing family secrets for the scrutiny of others is an enterprise that is shown to be double-edged in terms of its consequences for the writer-narrator. On the one hand, subjecting personal experience to the gaze of the other can lead to oppression and rejection. This is evident, for example, in the dismissal of Ernaux's family's 'habitus' (Bourdieu's term for an individual's social habits and beliefs) by members of the dominant social group, such as the daughter's schoolfriends and teachers. On the other hand, however, the adult narrator's act of writing about her past relationships and experiences, an act which renders hitherto private secrets public and implicitly invites the reader to make certain assessments and judgements about her family and her past, is often described as a potentially liberating activity. Writing about the father's violence appears to allow the narrator of *La Honte*, for example, to move beyond the imprisoning sense of shame that she claims surrounded her sense of self in her formative years. In this chapter I shall discuss, first, the ways in which Ernaux's family members, and her younger self, are subjected to the judgemental gaze of the other, and are made to feel ashamed of the 'secret' realities of their everyday lives. Second, I shall explore the ways in which writing about family secrets ultimately allows Ernaux's narrator to escape such judgements, especially in *La Honte*, and to construct a self no longer defined solely by shame and guilt.

Ernaux's texts are full of incidents in which the daughter is made aware of her family's failings. I have discussed in previous chapters, for instance, the episode in *La Place* in which the narrator's father is judged by his local librarians when he is unable to name a book he would like to take out: 'A la maison, on n'avait pas pensé qu'il fallait savoir d'avance ce qu'on voulait, être capable de citer des titres aussi facilement que des marques de biscuits. On a choisi à notre place, *Colomba* pour moi, un roman *léger* de Maupassant pour mon père' (*4*, p.112). This incident equally dramatises the way in which the values of the dominant social group are internalised by those they deem to be inferior. The father meekly submits to his treatment, and does not return to the library, thus confirming the librarians' implicit judgement about his lower social status. The process of internalisation of the values of the dominant class is, however, most evident in the figure of the daughter. As a schoolgirl, she begins to conceal certain aspects of her parents' habits and behaviour when she realises that exposing them to her peers and teachers will lead to mockery and condemnation. In *La Place*, for example, after outlining the working-class culture and habits that her father has retained from his rural background, the narrator remarks: 'Ce portrait, j'aurais pu le faire autrefois, en rédaction, à l'école, si la description de ce que je connaissais n'avait pas été interdite' (*4*, p.69). She learns along with her lessons, in other words, that it is unacceptable to tell the truth about her family life, as it contravenes the rules of seemly behaviour at her school. Her loyalties begin to be painfully divided as she is forced to choose between valuing the ideology she absorbs from her school, that condemns her parents' existence as inferior, and continuing to accept the values, behavioural norms and expectations of her home life. As I illustrate in Chapter 2, as the daughter proceeds up the educational ladder it is the values of the higher social classes that ultimately win out, and she comes to reject her parents (particularly her father) and their way of life: 'Je lui faisais des remarques sur sa façon de manger ou de parler. J'aurais eu honte de lui reprocher de ne pas pouvoir m'envoyer en vacances, j'étais sûre qu'il était légitime de vouloir le faire changer de manières. Il aurait peut-être préféré avoir une autre fille' (*4*, p.82).

One of the ways in which the narrator becomes conscious of the 'inferiority' of her home life is via the condemnatory gaze of others. Ernaux draws attention to the extent to which the critical middle-class gaze is a key agent of social oppression. In *La Place*, the narrator's father is shown to be uncomfortably aware of his 'inferior' social status when being observed by those he considered socially superior:

> Devant les personnes qu'il jugeait importantes, il avait une raideur timide, ne posant jamais aucune question. Bref, se comportant avec intelligence. Celle-ci consistait à percevoir notre infériorité et à la refuser en la cachant du mieux possible. [...] Honte d'ignorer ce qu'on aurait forcément su si nous n'avions pas été ce que nous étions, c'est-à-dire inférieurs. Obsession: *"Qu'est-ce qu'on va penser de nous?"* (les voisins, les clients, tout le monde). (*4*, pp.60–61)

The above quotation makes it clear that the parents are not coerced into behaving in a certain way, but rather are self-regulatory when it comes to monitoring their behaviour. They often appear to accept the invalidity of their habits, language and milieu and attempt to hide the realities of their existence when confronted with the gaze of the middle classes. Their obsession with the way they are seen by other people, moreover, is presented as widespread in their milieu: 'Tout le monde surveillait tout le monde. Il fallait absolument connaître la vie des autres — pour la raconter — et murer la sienne — pour qu'elle ne le soit pas' (*11*, p.65). Giving the right outward impression and hiding one's secrets so as not to become a talking point in the community was evidently an unspoken rule in the narrator's family. This need for secrecy has important consequences for the unsayable and unspeakable nature of the scene of her father's violence that the narrator witnesses as a twelve-year-old, and that forms the kernel of *La Honte*. As Lawrence Kritzman comments: 'The daughter saw the unveiling of the family secret as a violation of the code of privacy (her parents believed it violated a personal ethic) and a betrayal of parental trust' (*43*, p.140). Not only is the scene unacceptable in terms of the ideology she learns at school, but equally exposing it to public view is unacceptable in terms of her parents' determination to 'murer [leur vie]', to draw a firm line between public and private, in order to not lay themselves open to criticism or ridicule via the condemnatory gaze of the other.

An essential factor in the daughter's internalisation of a sense of shame about her family's social inferiority, and her desire to mask or hide certain aspects of their behaviour, is the Catholic ideology that permeates her school. As Philippe Vilain points out, Catholicism has consistently played a central role in Ernaux's representation of social and sexual shame: 'L'idéologie chrétienne est comme infusée dans le comportement des narratrices [dans l'œuvre d'Annie Ernaux], dans leur silence et leurs réticences, qui sont autant d'indices susceptibles de nous renseigner sur la sexualité d'une jeune fille vivant en milieu populaire autour des années 50' (*62*, p.153). *La Honte* is no exception in this respect. Religion and education are presented in *La Honte* as being inextricably intertwined in the narrator's girls' school: 'L'enseignement et la religion ne sont séparés ni dans l'espace ni dans le temps. Tout, sauf la cour de récréation et les cabinets, est lieu de prière' (*11*, p.80). Lessons begin and end with prayers, the classrooms are adorned with crucifixes on the walls, and the schoolgirls go regularly from their lessons to confession and communion. The structure of the school day is also prescribed according to a Catholic agenda: 'Le temps scolaire est inscrit dans un autre temps, celui du missel et de l'évangile, qui détermine la nature du thème de l'instruction religieuse quotidienne précédant la dictée' (*11*, p.83). The Catholic private school sets the narrator apart from her parents and from other family members, as she was the only one not to attend a state school. The distinction between the 'école privée' and the 'école publique' is marked in numerous ways by the school itself. The terms used for everyday items, for example, deliberately sets her school apart from secular establishments: 'On ne dit pas la "cantine" mais le "réfectoire", ni le "portemanteau" mais la "patère". "Camarades" et "maîtresse" sentent le laïc, il convient de dire "mes compagnes" et "mademoiselle", appeler la directrice "ma chère sœur"' (*11*, p.85). The school is a closed world (it is telling in this context that 'rien du pensionnat n'était visible du dehors': *11*, p.76), and has its own set of immutable rules. Few men other than priests are allowed to enter, and the nuns and female teachers in charge of the female pupils constantly emphasise the need for piety, modesty, obedience and purity. The exemplars of human behaviour and relationships promoted by the school were thus far removed from those the narrator encountered at home. More familiar than the pupils' own genealogy, for instance, was that of the protagonists of Christian theology:

> D'année en année, chaque jour, l'école privée nous fait revivre la même histoire et nous entretient dans la familiarité de personnages invisibles et omniprésents, ni morts ni vivants, les anges, la Sainte Vierge, l'Enfant Jésus, dont nous connaissons mieux la vie que celle de nos grands-parents. (*11*, p.83)

Catholic doctrine is presented as having permeated the very fabric of the narrator's childhood thoughts and beliefs. It offered her a model of transcendent flawlessness — 'le monde de la vérité et de la perfection, de la lumière' (*11*, p.85) — against which to judge her thoughts, appearance and actions, as well as those of others.

Although the narrator states that at the time it did not feel like 'un ordre coercitif' (*11*, p.90), the Catholic ideology she absorbs at

her school effectively renders many aspects of her life 'impure' and
shameful, in that they fail to measure up to the impossible ideals of
purity and perfection that are propagated in her school. Significant
in this respect is the description in *La Honte* of Mlle L., an
extremely strict nun and teacher who is feared and respected by
pupils and parents alike. The narrator tells us that Mlle L. became a
kind of touchstone against which she measured her own behaviour:
'C'est à elle que je me mesure, plus qu'aux autres élèves […]. Je
prends son acharnement à traquer mes imperfections scolaires
comme une manière de me faire accéder à sa propre perfection' (*11*,
p.95). Despite the narrator's excellent academic performance, Mlle
L. constantly finds fault with her mannerisms and habits, criticising
for example the way she forms the letter 'm' in her handwriting:

> Un jour elle m'a reproché la forme de mes "m", dont je
> recourbe le premier jambage vers l'intérieur à la façon
> d'une trompe d'éléphant, ricanant "*cela fait vicieux*".
> J'ai rougi sans rien dire. Je savais ce qu'elle voulait me
> signifier, et elle savait que je le savais: "Vous dessinez
> le *m* comme un sexe d'homme". (*11*, pp.95–96)

The fact that the narrator's apparent 'failing' is related to the male
body, and to sexuality, is particularly telling. *La Honte* emphasises
the extent to which Catholic doctrine focuses on the spiritual,
cerebral aspects of life, and condemns anything associated with
human sexuality, or simply with the functions of the human body, as
potentially sinful. This is apparent in the description of the exposed
mother's body when the daughter returns late from a school trip
with her teacher and school friends that, as I argue in previous
chapters, is a key episode in *La Honte* (*11*, p.117). It is the sight of
the mother's body, and the evidence of her 'unseemly' habit of
wiping herself with her nightgown after urinating, that causes the
greatest degree of shame in the daughter — especially as at other
points in the narrative the mother functions as a model of female
behaviour that she admires. Recognising and, at least to some
extent, sharing the horrified gaze of her teacher and peers makes the

adolescent acutely aware that her family do not belong to the purity
and perfection of the timeless and bodiless Catholic 'family' into
which her school has welcomed her. The mother's degraded, abject
body is placed in direct contrast to the understated and apparently
sexless body of Mlle L.: 'Elle est petite [...] plate et agitée, d'âge
indéfinissable, avec un chignon gris, une face ronde et des verres
grossissants qui lui font des yeux énormes. Comme toutes les
religieuses en civil, elle porte sur sa blouse en hiver une pèlerine à
rayures bleues et noires' (*11*, p.93). The teacher is associated with
the spiritual and cerebral, and with Catholic representation of
virginal purity. In relation to what Lawrence Kritzman terms the
'abstract ideal transmitted by the figure of the schoolteacher' (*43*,
p.145), the mother is made to represent the degraded earthliness of
human flesh. In sum, despite the mother's adherence to the tenets of
Catholic doctrine — 'Ma mère est le relais de la loi religieuse et des
prescriptions de cette école' (*11*, p.107) — her exposed body is
condemned by the critical gaze of the teacher and pupils from the
Catholic school. Further, the shame provoked by the sight of the
mother's body is clearly related to the father's violence with which
the narrative opens (they are both described using the term 'scène').
Indeed, as Nancy Miller persuasively argues, the former is
potentially more effective in its dramatisation of the extent to which
sexuality and the body were taboo in the narrator's childhood
milieu:

> The scene [...] homes in [...] on a body unprotected by
> constraint — the body at its most revealing, not naked
> but not veiled either. The body makes visible what
> remained hidden by the traumatic assault upon the
> mother in the basement. Now the shame is visible —
> like a wound — to the look of the outsider, the look she
> wishes as a writer to find unbearable. (*48*, p.45)

The exposure of the mother's body and the daughter's witnessing of
the father's murderous rage both make visible the 'impure' nature
of her parents' behaviour, intimately related to sexuality and to the

human body. (It is notable in this respect that the narrator associates the scene of the father's violence with her parents' sexuality, commenting: 'Mes parents ont peut-être évoqué entre eux la scène du dimanche, le geste de mon père, trouvé une explication, ou une excuse, et décidé de tout oublier. Par exemple, une nuit après avoir fait l'amour': *11*, p.21.) It is the very act of *seeing* the evidence of her parents' belonging to the earthly sphere of 'sinful flesh' rather than to the cerebral, spiritual world promoted by her 'école privée' that leaves the daughter with a feeling of guilt, of having in some way lost her purity and innocence:

> Nous avons cessé d'appartenir à la catégorie des gens corrects, qui ne boivent pas, ne se battent pas, s'habillent proprement pour aller en ville. [...] Je ne ressemblais plus aux autres filles de la classe. J'avais vu ce qu'il ne fallait pas voir. Je savais ce que, dans l'innocence sociale de l'école privée, je n'aurais pas dû savoir et qui me situait de façon indicible dans le camp de ceux dont la violence, l'alcoolisme ou le dérange-ment mental alimentaient les récits conclus par "c'est tout de même malheureux de voir ça". (*11*, pp.115–16)

It is thus not only class dynamics that render the private details of the narrator's life in *La Honte* shameful when they are exposed to the gaze of the other. Equally as important is the powerful gaze of the Church, embodied by her teachers, by the priests, by the religious statues in her school, and occasionally (and paradoxically) by her mother, that places the narrator's family secrets in the category of the sinful and the socially unacceptable.

Yet despite the oppressive aspects of the Catholic doctrine that makes the narrator of *La Honte* feel that she has become 'indigne de l'école privée, de son excellence et de sa perfection' (*11*, p.116), the escape route out of her prison of shame as an adult writer closely resembles the most Catholic of occupations, that of the confession. The narrative of *La Honte* is set up from the outset as a confessional text. We are told: 'J'écris cette scène pour la première fois. Jusqu'à aujourd'hui, il me semblait impossible de le faire, même dans un journal intime. Comme une action interdite devant entraîner un châtiment' (*11*, p.16). The 'unnarratable' and shameful nature of speaking out about the father's violence is confirmed by Ernaux herself in recent interview: 'Lorsque j'ai commencé, en 1990, le texte que j'appellerai ultérieurement *La Honte* il s'agissait pour moi d'écrire ce qu'il serait le plus difficile et le plus "dangereux" d'écrire' (*26*, p.145). In exposing what was previously the darkest of secrets, Ernaux casts the reader as a kind of priest, offering understanding and absolution to the confessing sinner. Thus, importantly, *La Place* and *La Honte* do not only illustrate the humiliating consequences of revealing family secrets to the condemnatory gaze of the socially 'superior'. They also focus on the effects of exposing such secrets to the reader, who as an anonymous receiver of the narrator's tale renders the act of confession a potentially more liberating enterprise, offering catharsis rather than condemnation.

In the opening sections of *La Honte*, the narrator emphasises the initial difficulty she experienced in expressing in words the scene of her father's violence. Jennifer Willging argues in her study of *La Honte* that Ernaux's text manifests the signs of deep psychological trauma. For Willging, Ernaux's narrator resembles a traumatised individual who is unable to communicate his/her experience:

> What the traumatized individual remembers [...] are images, textures, smells, sounds, and emotions. [...] Specifically missing from these memories are words, which would render the event not only understandable — that is, graspable not just by the body but also by the intellect as well — but also communicable. These kinds of memories, sensory memories, are what *La Honte*'s narrator has principally retained of the scene between her parents. (*63*, p.88)

It is sounds rather than words that the narrator remembers when recounting the scene, such as the father's 'voix rauque' and the mother's (or perhaps daughter's) 'sanglots' and 'cris' (*11*, p.15). What the adult narrator is attempting to do, therefore, is to construct a narrative out of the wordless impressions — 'la terreur sans mots' (*11*, p.21) — that formed her memories of the event as a child. In so doing, a key aim is to render the episode meaningful, so it can be integrated into her life rather than standing detached as an iconic 'scène' impossible either to discuss or comprehend. In this sense, the act of autobiographical writing performs a similar function in both *La Place* and *La Honte*. In the former, writing allows the daughter-narrator to reconnect to her past and to her family's milieu, thereby diminishing the gulf that separated her from her parents as a result of her education and entry into a higher social class. In *La Honte*, writing is also viewed as having the potential to act as a means of integrating previously disconnected elements of the narrator's life into a more coherent whole. The aim is to reinsert the self who experienced the scene, who is represented by the pious girl in the communion photograph, into the rest of the narrator's life story. Such a reintegration is necessary as, in Ernaux's œuvre, something that is seen to be 'outside' language, to be beyond words, is viewed in highly negative terms, representing a schism or 'wound' in the narrator's sense of self. Narrating the previously unnarratable, in confessional or therapeutic mode, can therefore result in a more integrated and satisfying sense of self. Chloe Taylor Merleau summarises this aspect of Ernaux's writing in the following terms:

> Something without words or name is terrifying, just as trauma is said to be experienced as outside of language, and healed through it. According to Ernaux, writing, a process of finding names and words for experiences, renders something that seemed beyond language, and hence extraordinary, into something containable, externalised, and, to some degree, normalised. (*57*, p.4)

Viewed in this light, the consequences of exposing secrets to the reader are much more positive in terms of the narrator's sense of self than the lack of self-worth and shame she derives from exposing them to the accusatory gaze of the middle classes. Rather, they give her the possibility of healing, through language, a self wounded by past psychological trauma.

These positive consequences of finally writing about the father's violence are made evident in the last scene of *La Honte*, in which the narrator looks again at the photograph taken on holiday in Biarritz. As a result of having 'confessed' her social and sexual shame, the narrator no longer feels confined by the same ideological bonds of Catholic dogma that condemned 'the sins of the flesh':

> Je n'ai plus rien de commun avec la fille de la photo, sauf cette scène du dimanche de juin qu'elle porte dans la tête et qui m'a fait écrire ce livre, parce qu'elle ne m'a jamais quittée. C'est elle seulement qui fait de cette petite fille et de moi la même, puisque l'orgasme où je ressens le plus mon identité et la permanence de mon être, je ne l'ai connu que deux ans après. (*11*, p.142)

Here, the adult narrator is able to cut the ties that once bound her to the fearful adolescent of the photograph, and rejoice in her sense of social and sexual confidence, finally embracing her sexuality as one of the key elements of her identity (something, notably, that her mother is not seen to have been able to do).

In this sense, the 'confession' or 'therapy' that constitutes the text of *La Honte* has successfully performed its healing function, allowing the narrator to move forward after having in Merleau's terms 'externalised', 'contained' and 'normalised' the scene of her father's violence — a scene that functioned as a cipher for the crippling sense of social and sexual shame that permeated her childhood. Yet, finally, we should hesitate before drawing such a positive conclusion from the narrator's exposure of her family secrets in *La Honte*. We are told that the narrator had actually previously confessed the murder scene to a number of lovers, and that this telling of the secret had not succeeded in ridding it of its iconic status (*11*, p.16). It is true that the reader can be understood potentially to have a more sympathetic ear than her lovers, who did not wish to hear her story of domestic violence. But it is equally true that Ernaux has not ceased in her work to return to episodes in her past, to repeat the scenes of trauma that scarred her childhood identity. As Merleau notes: 'Ernaux draws attention to the fact that although each book claims to have been a process of healing, later books show that the wounds are not healed, and the patterns of behaviour are not left behind' (*63*, p.6). In *La Honte*, the narrator makes a number of important discoveries. She learns that the scene of her father's rage was not in itself responsible for her feelings of shame. She thereby unveils a truth about her father that she was initially unable to access via her personal recollections, and is able, to some extent, to rewrite the *histoire* of their relationship, incorporating a new understanding of the fundamental importance of the social and religious discourses that she unconsciously absorbed as a twelve-year-old girl. Yet she equally suggests that this is not the final word on her past, or on her relationship with her father. As I noted in my Introduction, this belief in the inability of a single written text to convey the complete or final 'truth' of an individual or of the past is a crucial element of Ernaux's autobiographical project, and one which is consistently demonstrated throughout *La Place* and *La Honte*.

Bibliography

WORKS BY ERNAUX

1. *Les Armoires vides* (Paris: Gallimard, 1974)
2. *Ce qu'ils disent ou rien* (Paris: Gallimard, 1977)
3. *La Femme gelée* (Paris: Gallimard, 1981)
4. *La Place* (Paris: Gallimard, 1983)
5. *La Place*, introduction by P.M.Wetherill (London: Methuen Educational, 1987)
6. *Une femme* (Paris: Gallimard, 1988)
7. *Passion simple* (Paris: Gallimard, 1991)
8. *Journal du dehors* (Paris: Gallimard, 1993)
9. 'Fragments autour de Phillipe V.', *L'Infini* 56 (1996), 25–26
10. *'Je ne suis pas sortie de ma nuit'* (Paris: Gallimard, 1997)
11. *La Honte* (Paris: Gallimard, 1997)
12. *L'Evénement* (Paris: Gallimard, 2000)
13. *La Vie extérieure* (Paris: Gallimard, 2000)
14. *Se perdre* (Paris: Gallimard, 2001)
15. *L'Occupation* (Paris: Gallimard, 2002)
16. (with Marc Marie), *L'Usage de la photo* (Paris: Gallimard, 2005)

ESSAYS BY ERNAUX

17. 'Vers un je transpersonnel', *Cahiers RITM: Autofictions et cie* 6 (1993), 219–23
18. 'Texte d'Annie Ernaux', in *Acteurs du siècle*, preface by Bernard Thibault (Paris: Editions Cercle d'Art, 2000), pp.43–53
19. 'Le fil conducteur qui me lie à Beauvoir', *Simone de Beauvoir Studies* 17 (2000–2001), 1–6
20. 'Bourdieu, le chagrin', *Le Monde*, 6 Feb 2002, p.16
21. *L'Ecriture comme un couteau, entretien avec Frédéric-Yves Jeannet* (Paris: Stock, 2003)
22. 'Sur l'écriture', *LittéRéalité* 15 (2003), 9–22

INTERVIEWS WITH ERNAUX

23. Michèle Bacholle, 'An interview with Annie Ernaux: Ecrire le vécu', *Sites* 2 (1998), 141–51

24. Pierre-Louis Fort, 'Entretien avec Annie Ernaux', *French Review* 76 (2003), 984–94

25. Claire-Lise Tondeur, 'Entretien avec Annie Ernaux', *French Review* 69 (1995), 37–45

26. Philippe Vilain: 'Entretien: Annie Ernaux ou l'autobiographie en question', *Roman 20–50* 24 (1997), 141–47

27. Philippe Vilain, 'Entretien avec Annie Ernaux: une "conscience malheureuse" de femme', *LittéRéalité* 9 (1997), 111–13

CRITICAL WORKS ON ERNAUX

28. 'L'Autobiographie selon Annie Ernaux', special issue of *L'Ecole des lettres* 9 (2003)

29. Michèle Bacholle, *Un passé contraignant: Double bind et transculturation* (Amsterdam: Rodopi, 2000)

30. Michèle Bacholle, 'Confessions d'une femme pudique: Annie Ernaux', *French Forum* 28 (2003), 91–109

31. Sarah Cant, 'The Writer and the Representation of Experience in Annie Ernaux's *La Honte*', in *French Prose in 2000*, ed. by Michael Bishop and Christopher Elson (Amsterdam: Rodopi, 2002), pp.249–57

32. Michèle Chossat, *Ernaux, Redonnet, Bâ et Ben Jelloum: le personnage féminin à l'aube du XXIème siècle* (New York: Peter Lang, 2002)

33. Loraine Day, 'Revisioning the "Matricidal" Gaze: The Dynamics of the Mother/Daughter Relationship in Annie Ernaux's *"Je ne suis pas sortie de ma nuit"* and *La Honte*', *Dalhousie French Studies* 51 (2000), 150–73

34. Loraine Day and Tony Jones, *Ernaux, La Place and Une femme* (Glasgow: University of Glasgow French and German Publications, 1990)

35. Loraine Day and Lyn Thomas, 'Exploring the interspace: Recent dialogues around the work of Annie Ernaux', *Feminist Review* 74 (2003), 98–104

36. Christine Fau, 'Le Problème du langage chez Annie Ernaux', *French Review* 68 (1995), 501–12

37. Alison S. Fell, *Liberty, Equality, Maternity in Beauvoir, Leduc and Ernaux* (Oxford: Legenda, 2003)

38. Alison S. Fell, 'Recycling the Past: Annie Ernaux's evolving *écriture de soi*', *Nottingham French Studies* 41 (2002), 60–69

39. Denis Fernandez-Recatala, *Annie Ernaux* (Monaco: Editions de Rocher, 1994)

40. Christian Garaud, 'Ecrire la différence sociale: registres de vie et registres de langue dans *La Place* d'Annie Ernaux', *French Forum* 29 (1994), 196–214

41. Diana Holmes, 'Feminism and Realism: Christiane Rochefort and Annie Ernaux', in Diana Holmes, *French Women's Writing 1848– 1994* (London: Athlone Press, 1996), pp.246–65

42. Warren Johnson, 'The Dialogic Self: Language and Identity in Annie Ernaux', *Studies in Twentieth-Century Literature* 23 (1999), 297–314

43. Lawrence D. Kritzman, 'Ernaux's Testimony of Shame', *L'Esprit créateur* 39 (1999), 139–50

44. Bethany Ladimer, 'Cracking the Codes: Social Class and Gender in Annie Ernaux', *Chimères: A Journal of French Literature* 26 (2002), 53–69

45. Siobhan McIlvanney, *Annie Ernaux: The Return to Origins* (Liverpool: Liverpool University Press, 2001)

46. Siobhan McIlvanney, 'Writing Relations: The auto/biographical subject in Annie Ernaux's *La Place* and *Une femme*', *Journal of the Institute of Romance Studies* 7 (1999), 205–15

47. Tony McNeill, 'Annie Ernaux: *La Place*', www.sunderland.ac.uk/~os0tmc/contem/er2.htm Accessed 13 July 2005

48. Nancy K. Miller, 'Memory Stains: Annie Ernaux's *Shame*', *a/b: Auto/Biography Studies* 14 (1999), 38–50

49. Nathalie Morello, '"Faire pour la mère ce qu'elle [n']avait [pas] fait pour le père": étude comparative du projet autobiographique dans *La Place* et *Une femme* d'Annie Ernaux', *Nottingham French Studies* 38 (1999), 80–92

50. Warren Motte, 'Annie Ernaux's Understatement', *French Review* 69 (1995), 55–65

51. Annie Olivier, 'Ecritures de femmes et autobiographie: *La Place* de Annie Ernaux', *Studi Francesi* 46 (2002), 391–407

52. Thierry Poyet, '*La Place* d'Annie Ernaux: Pour une definition du rapport entre la forme et le lectorat', *L'Ecole des lettres* 9 (2003), 37–49

53. Christian Roche, 'Trahison et littérature dans *La Place* d'Annie Ernaux', *Women in French Studies* 7 (1999), 132–42

54. Carol Sanders, 'Stylistic aspects of women's writing: the case of Annie Ernaux', *French Cultural Studies* 4 (1993), 15–29

55. Marie-France Savéan, *La Place et Une femme d'Annie Ernaux* (Paris: Gallimard Foliothèque, 1994)

56. Michael Sheringham, 'Invisible Presences: Fiction, Autobiography and Women's Lives: Virginia Woolf to Annie Ernaux', *Sites* 2 (1998), 5–24

57. Chloë Taylor Merleau, 'The Confessions of Annie Ernaux: Autobiography, Truth and Repetition', *Journal of Modern Literature* 28 (2005), 65–88

58. Lyn Thomas, *Annie Ernaux: An Introduction to the Writer and her Audience* (Oxford: Berg, 1999)

59. Fabrice Thumerel (ed.), *Annie Ernaux: une œuvre de l'entre-deux* (Arras: Artois Presses Université, 2004)

60. Claire-Lise Tondeur, *Annie Ernaux ou l'exil intérieur* (Amsterdam: Rodopi, 1996)

61. Claire-Lise Tondeur, 'Ecrire la honte (Annie Ernaux)', in *French Prose in 2000*, ed. by Michael Bishop and Christopher Elson (Amsterdam: Rodopi, 2002), pp.125–35

62. Philippe Vilain, 'Le sexe et la honte dans l'œuvre d'Annie Ernaux', *Roman 20–50: Revue d'étude du roman du XXe siècle* 24 (1997), 149–64

63. Jennifer Willging, 'Annie Ernaux's Shameful Narration', *French Forum* 26 (2001), 83–103